The Seven Gateways of Spiritual Experience

"Jonathan Ellerby's experience-rich new book is full of heart and a timely way to wake up to our full nature. *The Seven Gateways of Spiritual Experience* offers us a roadmap to ways we can dive into spiritual knowing as well as discover the inner resources we each have and integrate them into our thinking and choices. Enter into the world of possibilities Jonathan unfolds and explore your own abilities to connect with The Sacred. A wonderful guide to ancient and new ways of knowing."

— **Ellen Meredith, D.A., EEMAP**, energy medicine practitioner and author of *Your Body Will Show You the Way*

"In this book, the reader will feel an overflowing of hope, love, mysticism, and beauty. Jonathan fills the pages with his compelling storytelling gifts. Reading this book is like setting out on a real and ethereal excursion, and Jonathan invites all to travel with him. Not accepting the invitation into Jonathan's journey is not an option because his writing is from deep within his heart and the desire to join him is palpable and unavoidable. All who read *The Seven Gateways of Spiritual Experience* will feel Jonathan's profound vision on every page. It is likely you'll find yourself mesmerized."

— **Steve Farrell**, cofounder and CEO of Humanity's Team and author of *A New Universal Dream*

"Jonathan's guide on experiences of The Sacred feels like an answer to what so many seekers and students of transformation and consciousness are looking for. Profound in its depth and range of perspectives on the spiritual life, this book is wonderfully written, heart- and mind-opening, and a true spiritual experience to read."

~ **Steven Washington**, dancer, Qigong and Pilates instructor, and author of *Recovering You: Soul Care and Mindful Movement for Overcoming Addiction*

"I love this book! It opens the heart and mind and reminds us that we are all capable of profound love and wisdom—we are spiritual beings first. Jonathan Ellerby is the real deal! From direct experience to deep study, years of leadership, and the academic credentials to support this work, he is a visionary to follow and a wonderful guide for all seekers of transformation."

~ **Dr. Ken Harris**, M.S., D.C., chiropractor, educator, and author of *Synchronicity: The Magic. The Mystery. The Meaning.*

THE SEVEN GATEWAYS OF
SPIRITUAL
EXPERIENCE

Awakening to a Deeper Knowledge of
Love, Life Balance, and God

Jonathan H. Ellerby, Ph.D.

FINDHORN PRESS

Findhorn Press
One Park Street
Rochester, Vermont 05767
www.findhornpress.com

Findhorn Press is a division of Inner Traditions International

Disclaimer

The information in this book is given in good faith and is neither intended
to diagnose any physical or mental condition nor to serve as a substitute
for informed medical advice or care. Please contact your health professional
for medical advice and treatment. Neither author nor publisher can be held
liable by any person for any loss or damage whatsoever which may arise
from the use of this book or any of the information therein.

Cataloging-in-Publication data for this title
is available from the Library of Congress

ISBN 978-1-64411-886-3 (print)
ISBN 978-1-64411-887-0 (ebook)

Printed and bound in the United States by Lake Book Manufacturing, LLC

10 9 8 7 6 5 4 3 2 1

Edited by Michael Hawkins
Text design and layout by Yasko Takahashi
This book was typeset in Garamond and Novel Sans
with FUD Grotesk used as a display typeface.

To send correspondence to the author of this book, mail a first-class letter
to the author c/o Inner Traditions • Bear & Company, One Park Street,
Rochester, VT 05767, USA and we will forward the communication, or
contact the author directly at **connect@jonathanellerby.com**.

For all those who have guided me along the way,
family, friends, masters, and those who continue
by my side: Uxia, Narayan, Aluxa & Juno.

I will never forget
That moment
It came and went like a falling star
In the darkest night sky
The world stood still
Time vanished and eternity breathed into me
I was lost in that moment
And I was free
Dissolving into an expanse
Beyond time
Beyond the sorrow that clutched at my life
Beyond the tangled mind and fading forms I created
To protect and guide
Everything vanished
And Everything was revealed
In that moment
There was no room for doubt
No room for decision
There was only the simple truth
Within me a depth beyond imagination
A strength that will carry me through
A light, a hope
And so much more.

Contents

Foreword

Since the moment I first heard Jonathan speak, I was intent on remaining skeptical and guarded. In pursuit of healing my own wounds with several teachers and mentors over the years, I'd recognized my reliance and blind trust of those further along on their spiritual path. My willingness to listen to another man's teachings about consciousness and personal growth surprised me. But when I heard his repeated affirmation to me that "everything I need can be found within," and saw that he embodies this in each aspect of his life, I slowly allowed Jonathan to become my teacher, spiritual mentor and trusted friend. All has unfolded within the parameters of authenticity, mutual respect, and reliance on my own growing awareness and inner knowing.

For decades, my fear of being fully present in the natural world had been paralyzing. During a group nature excursion led by Jonathan and through his one-on-one guidance, with great compassion and experienced challenging, he helped me find my will to surrender, step off my personal edge and confront my most painful fears.

One year later as he dropped me off on an uncharted, unoccupied, heavily wooded wilderness island for the day, my first hours spent fearlessly curled up under a pine tree sleeping, I welcomed a constant parade of creatures from land, water, air and beyond and found my own way into spiritual dimensions that have had no name until now. My newly formed relationship with the natural world has given me a voice and the confidence to pursue public speaking, group facilitation, and leading my own nature retreats.

I'd been given the opportunity to read Jonathan's most recent manuscript for *Spiritual Experience* and it was truly an honor. I'd borrowed his first book, *Return to the Sacred* from the library almost two years ago and months later had checked it out again, believing I hadn't finished it. But I had. What I sensed was missing was this manuscript which you now hold—an explanation of what occurred when he experienced his transcendent experiences of The Sacred. *Return to the Sacred* is Jonathan's narrative of his personal spiritual awakening; and how others can determine which of his twelve broadly defined spiritual paths that can be taken to begin one's own steps toward awakening.

This latest book, however, comes much closer to one that's been communicated from a collective knowing of which he is an active participant. There are many books, mostly "channeled," that have relayed bits of the information detailed so beautifully here, but none have the authenticity and first-hand knowledge of their own interactions within these spiritual dimensions; nor have other books provided the context and a deep understanding of what has actually been experienced. What Jonathan describes on these pages wasn't transcribed or told to him: he lived it! *That's what makes this new book so important and exciting.* There is a delineation between teaching people what is required to have an awakening and teaching people to recognize the true gifts of their awakening.

Jonathan's experiences of each dimension described in this book are unique to him. Something, nevertheless, occurs when one is confronted with a reflection of the truth of who we are without distortions or illusions. A deep recognition and remembrance reverberates throughout our entire being: one that becomes increasingly difficult to ignore. I have found myself revisiting my own spiritual experiences throughout the reading of this book with a new found appreciation for the journeys

I've taken so far and the exploration of further insights that have been waiting for me.

Jonathan has gained his credibility through the traditional pursuits of advanced degrees and trainings, apprenticeships and jobs that are fully documented in his public biography and other books—and that matters greatly. But the ultimate proof for me comes down to the way his life experiences have shaped the man I know today; teacher, mentor, master facilitator, executive, nature guide, minister, healer, husband and father. In every case, he is consistent in his way of being. I personally know the hard work and discipline required to follow one's spiritual path. I am also familiar with the ramifications of experiencing other spiritual dimensions and the challenges of integrating them within one's daily life. I believe that without the accompanying inner and outer work prior to, and following, a life-expanding experience of the Divine, these pursuits are all for naught. Unlike other highly evolved beings, Jonathan's capacity to process and integrate his spiritual experiences is impeccable.

This book is a guide to accompany those who have chosen to walk their own spiritual journey. Each chapter describes the other-worldly dimensions we may find ourselves in. It provides a way to understand what is experienced and how its gifts and lessons can be integrated within one's self and world. No longer are we relegated to appreciate The Sacred second-hand through poets, musicians and artists. We are in receipt of guidance that doesn't refrain from describing how esoteric knowledge can be reached and brought back into the ordinary realms of our everyday life. This book is truly a rare and precious gift.

~ **Joni Klieger**, Integrative Energy Practitioner,
Denver, Colorado

Introduction

Anyone who has waded
Through Love's turbulent waters,
Now feeling hunger and now satiety,
Is untouched by the season
Of withering or blooming,
For in the deepest
And most dangerous waters,
On the highest peaks,
Love is always the same.

~ Hadewijch of Antwerp

Where Does Anything Begin?

Hadewijch of Antwerp, the author of the above poem, is a name that few find familiar, unlike the male mystics Rumi, Hafiz or Kabir. This potent 13th century French Beguine mystic has left a legacy much like other women of the time: powerful, vital, valuable, and mostly forgotten. Her personal story has never been recorded and we know little of her except by the extraordinary prose and poetry she left for us, like an overgrown forest trail leading back to the most intimate experiences of the Sacred one might imagine. What we do know is that she was quite literally "run out of town" for teaching people to trust their own inner and direct experience of the Sacred. Hadewijch knew that the church and all its teachers and teachings were mere human trappings and that each and anyone could come to know God intimately and personally. More so, Hadewijch assured her students, as documented in letters we still have copies of, that such deep spiritual experience is not a luxury for the elite or the privileged, but a vital root for a life of resilience and peace in difficult times.

Like the great Buddhist masters she writes, "You have to consider how you endure what opposes you and how you are able to go without things that are dear to you. . . Try and remain inwardly detached in all that happens to you: when you are troubled or when you enjoy peace of mind. And always contemplate the expressions of God, for these can teach you perfection." In this way, this master teacher understands that spiritual experience is anything but "woo-woo" idealism or a fantasy world believed only by some, but instead is an ultimately real endlessly solid foundation from which to build a life, face challenges, and bring peace to oneself and the world.

Much like Hadewijch and other women mystics and masters throughout time, the importance of direct personal spiritual experience has been overshadowed by the very masculine pursuits of correct belief, right understanding, competitive practice, and highly stratified and socialized belonging. While the world absolutely needs the gifts

of men and the masculine mind, it has suffered the loss of the feminine force and in the world of wellness and spiritual growth experience and embodied knowing, which I see as feminine paths, have been
pushed back into the shadow of the idealized experiences of experts
and authors.

Privilege and Power on the Spiritual Path

In light of this, I acknowledge that this book is overflowing with my
own stories and personal lived experiences of the Sacred. They must
not be idealized or envied. I share personal accounts to provide an
inside feeling for what each type of experience discussed might be like
for you and how you may recognize such things. These accounts are
samples of my own experiences and you must take the journey to find,
make, and receive your own.

The great tragedy of religious and spiritual tradition lies in the way
those who intend to serve or are in positions of leadership and service
have diminished the importance of each and every human experience
of the Spiritual World. Texts and practices are *vehicles* for spiritual
experience, not end points or goals. A perfect pigeon pose in yoga, an
extreme endurance of sweat lodge heat, memorization of bible verses,
or faithful supplication five times a day at the mosque are all mere
cultural or ego activities if the heart and mind are not open to the
possibility of direct connection and the full embrace of the Love and
Wisdom at hand. We study and practice to open to something *more
and beyond* what we study or practice. The tools are there to open us
to that which we cannot go directly towards.

To embrace our tools and traditions with a heart for awakening
is itself a type of privilege and one you must claim. Most people in
the world have been conditioned to believe that one type of practice
or another are for some and not others. The influence of social ideas
shapes our spiritual world: we see few images of People of Color doing

yoga unless they are idealized Indian gurus; we see few images of military meditators; women attend workshops while men work; Popes are white; radicals are Muslim; New Agers are foolish and fair-weather. All of these are false and harmful ideas and stereotypes. I can only ask that as you read this book you keep your mind open to every possibility for yourself. Let nothing you have been told or known before this moment limit what you might be tomorrow—or tonight!

I can look back now and see that my privilege as a white male was to consider that the world of spiritual experience and the practices of the world were all at my disposal. I traveled the world with unintentional impunity and without fear that I might be stopped or denied entrance to whatever I might want. That is a privilege hard to impart. Yet, what I learned along the way, however, is that there are barriers and limits, racism and exclusivity everywhere and yes, against me too. This book contains many stories set in African and Indigenous communities, places where I might have been seen as the "enemy" at first glance. In the end, the only thing that opened the many doors you will discover within was the power of the heart and the willingness to be a vulnerable, dedicated student—sincerely open to listen and *not* know.

In this way, I share my experiences so that you might discover that there is an infinite world of love and wisdom present and waiting for you in this very moment. Right now. Should you close your eyes, seek a deeper stillness and ask without attachment, *this* very moment could open a door to another way of knowing you haven't yet considered.

Know Yourself, Know the World

Part of the great power and importance of experiencing the spiritual world is to not only connect you with answers to questions and healing for life's wounds, but it is a means to correct your vision. As we enter the world of spiritual experience, again and again, we begin to realize that our world, our experience of the world and our story about it is profoundly limited. As such, all the pain of life becomes small in the vastness of the universe and the universe beyond. Pain becomes a gateway to connect with the human condition and the remembering that we are never alone, and always connected. Our joys become richer in the light of spiritual experience as we start to see them as portals to life's true nature.

Self-concern, social approval, and the conditioning of culture are rarely to our benefit, especially when unconscious. To embrace and explore spiritual experience is to pull back the veils of life and see that we are much more than we have been told and that all our fears and enemies are mere illusions that keep us from the lived experience of knowing that we are loved, that there is enough and that we belong: all of us, to each other, and always.

By releasing our fixation on the material world and diving into the domain of the spiritual, we naturally gain a view of life that allows for more wholeness, forgiveness, endurance, and the beautiful discovery of interconnection. Deep spiritual experience not only heals the one having the experience, but it empowers us to become helpers and healers for the world around us. Ironically, the more I have come to feel and understand just how not-human I am, just how spirit-full and spiritual this world is, the more I feel safe and willing to love and embrace life as it is. To be fully human is an amazing and wonderful adventure.

In my 35 years of researching integrative health, healing spiritual wellness and spiritual growth, each and every day has only affirmed that a life grounded in and fed by spiritual experience is a life of beauty and resilience. My life has been far from perfect. I have experienced betrayal in relationships, setbacks and failures in business, divorce, financial highs and devastating lows. I have faced people's false adoration and overwhelming expectation of me as a teacher and blind, jealous hatred of me as a teacher. I have had businesses stolen from me and debts owed to me and never paid. I have lost my father at a young age and tasted so many shades of life's bitterness and blessings. What has kept my spirit bright and my heart open through it all has been my direct experiences of Spirit and the Spiritual World.

No matter what life on earth delivers, I know I am a visitor and my stay may be ended any day. I am uplifted and steadied by my connection to a dimension of our existence that is not limited by my bank account or my health. I know this is a journey of discovery, a life of learning. Whatever arises, if I face it with the help and context of spiritual experience then I know that every day will lead me deeper into a profound knowing of love and wisdom that nothing can shake or take.

If you open your heart and mind to the stories and experiences in this book, try your hand at it, take some risks, explore and listen and explore some more, you will uncover your own relationship to dimensions of life and self that will astonish and inspire you. In discovering the magic of the spiritual world, you will discover the magic in yourself. In exploring the infinite qualities of this thing we call "God" or "Spirit" you will know yourself anew, and find all of life and love living within you—right here, right now. This interrelationship between the eternal and the particular, the small and the all, the self and the Spirit is beautifully described in a letter by Hadewijch of Antwerp:

"[Through spiritual experience, God] shall teach you
what God is and with what wonderful sweet-
ness the one lover lives in the other
and so permeates the other
that they do not know themselves from each other.
But they possess each other in mutual delight,
mouth in mouth, heart in heart, body in body, soul in soul,
while a single divine nature flows through them both
and they both become one through each other,
yet remaining always themselves."

~ Hadewijch of Antwerp, translated by Oliver Davies

Chapter One

The Geography of Spiritual Experience
Seven Super-States of Consciousness

There are more things in heaven and earth,
Horatio, than are dreamt of in your
philosophy.

~ Shakespeare, *Hamlet*, Act I, Scene 5

It is important to expect nothing,
to take every experience, including the negative ones,
as merely steps on the path, and to proceed.

~ Ram Dass

What Is a Spiritual Experience?

I knew Pam before she lost her eyesight due to diabetes. Pam is an Elder and a wisdom keeper in an Indigenous American community I became a part of many, many years ago. Now aging and debilitated by her advancing illness, Pam experiences the world in a way she never did before. Though she moves slowly, and requires a great deal of help, she remains alert. We have all been amazed at the way her ability to read the "energy" of a person and "sense" the mood of a room has become so astute.

I recall sitting down beside her at a community event one day. We were listening to a speaker at a gathering.

When I sat down, I said nothing. I was simply listening to a man talking before the crowd. After about fifteen minutes Pam turned in my direction, her dark glasses focused off into the distance. "Jonathan," she clearly said, "could you go get me some water, please." I got up right away and headed to the water fountain. As I filled a cup for her, it struck me, "How did she know it was me beside her?" Later on, I asked her.

"Since I lost my eyesight almost two years ago, I find that I can see in a different way now. I can feel people's energy. I experience the way sound moves in a space, and sometimes I can even feel if someone is sick or in need of healing." She laughed, "My grandsons like to tease and test me. Someone will stand in front of me and they'll call out, 'Who's that grandma? Who's that?' They try to trick me, but in some ways I think I see more clearly now than I ever did."

I often think of that experience with Pam when people ask about spiritual experience. I wonder how would I describe a sunset to a person who was born blind? How would I explain the sounds of a symphony to a person born deaf? How would they describe to me the experiences they have of the subtle energies of vibration, touch, and energy—aspects of life we overlook because of the dominance of our senses? Describing a spiritual experience is by its very nature a challenging task.

Spiritual experiences involve senses and qualities distinct from all others. When there is no common experience, metaphor, inference, and symbol are the best we can do. In the face of this the rational mind raises doubt and suspicion. If we cannot measure it, how can it be? Pam's experiences in her blindness are as real as her experiences with sight. Her ability to know things through the felt-sense of energy and spirit are accurate and meaningful, but there is no way to prove what senses she is using or how. Pam's way of relating to the world *is* a spiritual experience. Every day she relates to the invisible presence within and between all things. This is truly seeing in a sacred way.

Spiritual experience involves the opening of the eyes of the soul. We learn to hear with the ears of the heart. We touch with our spirit. Spiritual experience is better taught by poets and musicians than scholars and scientists, but we have lost our will to listen and learn from the magical. We have forgotten how to be playful and vulnerable, we have lost the ability to be surprised and sensitive. Spiritual experience is about the awakening to the soul of the self and the soul of the world. During spiritual experience we encounter a non-ordinary way of seeing, feeling, and knowing. Many theories and frameworks have been created over the years to explain this. Many are based in psychology, theology, or neurology, but none have the complete answer. Experience is the best way to know your own spiritual personality and the unique ways you are able to connect with The Sacred.

The Extraordinary Ordinary

Years ago, I was traveling home from university during a winter break and found myself stuck at an airport somewhere in the middle of the United States. I recall the extreme frustration being trapped in limbo; my plane canceled and an alternative flight yet to be determined. I had no money for a hotel and dreaded being trapped in the airport for days. I made phone calls, I stood in lines, I begged, I demanded.

I missed my family and I didn't want to waste my precious winter holiday time sleeping in an airport when I could be at home visiting friends and family. I pushed the situation from every angle and finally recognized that the only thing I could do was wait, until new arrangements could be made. It would be hours before any option might come to pass.

I had placed so much expectation on that trip that when it did not go as planned I felt deeply disappointed and frustrated. My frantic state finally gave way to absolute exasperation. I simply resigned myself and gave in to my sense of hopelessness. Thinking and worrying did not bring me closer to a solution. Anger and sadness didn't do much good either. Totally aware of how powerless I was to effect any change, I felt like all I could do was give up.

Listlessly I dug into my hand bag for my Walkman—the predecessor to the iPod and MP3 players—and put on a recording of *La Bohème,* one of Puccini's most famous operas. *La Bohème* was one of those rare finds in life for me; just when I thought I'd never like opera, *La Bohème* caught my attention. It always opened my heart and lifted me to feelings of inspiration and rapture. Maybe you have an album that reliably moves you to a similar place? For me, it was a choice to listen to something that would connect me to the moment, and not distract me from my experience of it. The first song began slowly, as if holding a moment of suspense, as if something magical was about to take place. And it did.

The symphony surged and the perfect voices of the man and woman singing danced across a subtle but growing rhythm. I felt my own emotion melt into the melancholy of the sweet serenades. It was hard to tell where my drama ended and theirs began. Soon, I too was sailing over the surging sounds, their world, my world, as one world. Still walking through the airport, I was in the music and the music poured out into the world around me.

Everywhere I looked, every person, every facial expression, every step and gesture was in tune, in time with the music. I stopped dead in my tracks. I watched in amazement as the world flowed around me. Each unfolding story was perfect: the sad girl on the pay phone, the pompous business man selling his story to a young protégé; the family laughing, the couple sleeping.

Everything that felt like chaos a moment ago was in perfect harmony, perfect order. A rhythm, a pattern, like a slow motion ballet; everyone was perfect in their own roles, unique and alive in the act of living the script they had been handed. Each playing their part as only they could; each playing the part they were born to play.

In that moment there was nothing but the extraordinary sense that everything was exactly as it should be; the awareness that the highs and lows are not the obstacles of life, but the very stuff that life is made of. In that moment there was no perfect plan, there was no judgment of self or others, there was nowhere to be, except in that moment. I realized that nothing had to be fixed, no one had to be wrong and no one had to be right. It was simple and glorious. Totally unexpected, unplanned, and glorious.

There, in the most unlikely of moments, far from anything religious, the naked Spirit of Life revealed itself. In a moment of letting go, a moment of surrender, life reveals its inner beauty and it is clear how The Sacred permeates all things. It was such a powerful reminder that there is always beauty, wisdom, and design in the world, if only we have eyes to see it. Often, spiritual experience is no more complex than letting go of all we want to simply appreciate *what is*.

How Natural Is Spiritual Experience?

Spiritual experience is one of those terms that has become stereotyped and misconceived. Many religious communities have come to fear direct spiritual experience, and modern secular communities have come to ridicule them. Associated with psychedelics, paranormal phenomena, and altered states of consciousness, many people have become unsure of the safety and validity of such experiences. Yet, those who have become familiar with them, know them, to be among the most important and defining experiences of their lives.

When we do not have a spiritual context or explanation, we often call such experiences "peak experiences" or "highs." An incredible moment at an airport, like the one just described, could be dismissed by many as only a momentary pleasure, and not an indicator of a deeper world or a deeper way of being. Just as we can be convinced that spirituality lives in a building or under the authority of a few people, we can also be convinced that the extraordinary moments of our lives are indications of nothing more than passing emotions. These moments should not be overlooked. They can be savored, contemplated, and explored for growth and learning. The spiritual path calls us to re-examine the nature of perception and our reality.

In the Western world there is great diversity of opinion about the nature and cause of spiritual experience. In Eastern cultures the nature of spiritual experience is something that has long been described and documented in detail. Buddhist and Hindu traditions, for example, have elaborate inventories, frameworks and schools of thought devoted to the study and understanding of spiritual experience. Most date back thousands of years and show great complexity and detail. Sacred practices are designed to evoke these experience so that we may have direct awareness and knowledge of The Sacred.

When referring to "The Sacred," most people intuitively understand that we are referring to something of ultimate importance and influence on life. As we discuss spiritual experience, the term "Sacred" certainly carries that same meaning, but with specific reference to those forces, feelings and aspects of our universe that are understood to be from or relating to a reality that transcends our ordinary physical and psychological world. Many traditions use the term, "The Sacred" to refer to the wide and likely unlimited world of Spirit, consciousness, and subtle energy that exist in a hidden yet accessible dimension of Life. Each tradition has their own understanding of what is included within "The Sacred," such as God, angels, spirits, Ascended Masters and more. For our purposes, we include any and all "things" that can be discovered or indicated through spiritual experience: all expressions of this Living Energy Universe.

Many modern societies have lost a sense of the Sacred and learned to abuse altered states and the practices once revered. Recreational drugs like alcohol, coffee, and marijuana, are all commonly used to medicate unsatisfying lives or simply to enrich a moment. As a result they become mundane subjects and continue to provide ways to escape life rather than embrace it.

Without respect and intention, even the sources of spiritual experience can be corrupted. Societies and governments have found many reasons to seek to condemn or control communities and individuals in search of spiritual experience. Whether the Ghost Dance of Indigenous, American people during the settlement of the American west, or the LSD researchers in the 1960s, few governments have tolerated or supported liberal access to experiences that show us that true power and authority exists beyond the human realm and can never be controlled or regulated.

Just as the Chinese government has opposed the *Falun Gong* movement, which cultivates inner peace, moral action, and a regular spiritual practice, governments all over the world have tended to oppose radical creativity and free thinking. Most great spiritual leaders, from Jesus Christ to Martin Luther King, were perceived by some as radicals.

The very essence of spiritual experience leads to a perception of the world that is free from fear, the belief in hierarchy, and materialism. Sadly, most thriving societies, businesses, and governments are built on these qualities and rely on them as mechanisms to maintain power and control. Despite fear or resistance, spiritual experience persists throughout time because it is essential to who we are as human beings. Such experiences are healing, instructive and more common than most can imagine.

The ability of the "average" person to have unexpected and extraordinary experiences of The Sacred is not only possible, but frequent.

Concert goers can experience a euphoric sense of unity with the music, performers, and other fans. Lovers can experience blissful moments of surrender, unity, and timelessness. Chefs, artists, athletes, and even business professionals can experience flow states of high awareness, connection, and creative insight. Even a sunset walk with your best friend or pet can deliver us into moments of sublime peace, openness to beauty, and a confidence in the hidden design of life. Though fleeting, we all have experiences that are not only filled with inexplicable feeling, but also meaning. The more people I meet and work with the more I am amazed at the profound and diverse ways people are experiencing the Spiritual World without even knowing it. What seems to make a significant difference in their lives is whether they recognize and integrate their experiences or not. This is often an issue of awareness, assumptions, and choice.

Frequently, this is also an issue that relates to religion and a lacking sense of permission to be independently spiritual. A surprising number of people feel that if they have a spiritual experience outside of a religious setting it must be wrong, or invalid. As with most things in life, people want a sense of permission. Again, the mind and "persona" get in the way. If we let the mind alone dictate what is true, then anything that defies logic or measure is received with less weight and meaning.

Powerful dreams, intuitive knowledge, the perception of subtle energies, a sense of being connected to something greater, astounding synchronicity, and the feeling of a guiding divine presence are all examples of extraordinarily ordinary experiences. Nevertheless, I have met many people in the USA and Canada who come to me with questions about spiritual experiences filled with guilt, shame, confusion, and fear. If they don't know what it is they are experiencing they often doubt or resist it. If their culture has not approved it, they assume it must be bad. Sadly, many children are chastised or educated not to pay attention to or respect their spiritual experiences.

Traveling in places like Asia, South America, Africa, and Native America, I have found that spiritual experiences, such as encounters with spiritual beings, transformative dreams, the power of faith, and the deep impact of intuition, are not only common, but expected. Rather than doubting, questioning, or denying such experiences, many cultures live with them and integrate them as a routine aspect of life. In most of these traditions, people understand the value of seeking these experiences. In such cultures, spiritual experience is a very real and necessary part of understanding human nature, our world, and the invisible Spiritual Worlds that lie beyond ordinary perception.

Though spiritual experiences are often profound and inconceivable, simple things like inspiration, a deep sense of hope, and the feeling of meaning or purpose can all be considered spiritual experiences. They help form the very foundations of our lives and choices. Regardless of belief or perspective, spiritual experience is essential to our health and a full experience of life. The secret lies in allowing the spiritual experiences, recognizing them, reflecting on them, and drawing their wisdom and peace into our daily lives. Just because it doesn't fit our religious upbringing, or what we've been told to expect does not mean it is not spiritual or meaningful. None of us were born knowing how to run, talk, or dance, and yet with very little encouragement and an environment of support, all such expressions come easily. Sometimes we just need a little support, or someone to help us see how spiritually connected we really are.

Not too long ago I met a woman who wanted to talk to me about her struggle entering a new phase of life. Cindy was nearing her fiftieth birthday, and was having second thoughts about her career. She talked about wanting to manage her constant stress better. She also confessed that she felt conflicted about her spiritual life and that it was bothering her. She felt she should be more peaceful and wanted to bring more "spirituality" into her life.

I asked what spirituality meant to her. She immediately expressed guilt and self-doubt. Then she went on for some time about her Catholic upbringing and shared her feeling of shame over not being more ardent in her faith. Her mood changed quickly as she went on to describe how she spends much of her time exploring her deep love of nature and animals. Moreover, she expressed her dedication to these things through acts of service and a lifestyle that promotes the restoration of the natural world and the healing of her community.

Cindy was most aglow when she talked about riding horses. Finally, she joked, "I wish that could be my spirituality. I don't often feel God in church, but out there in the open fields I feel something amazing. It is everywhere and within me. I feel so alive, the world feels so alive!"

She added, "Too bad that isn't religion."

"Why not?" I replied. "Why can't that be your spirituality?" I certainly affirm the value and importance of a religious community, but never at the exclusion of the direct connection to The Sacred—that would be ironically ridiculous. I stressed that her love of nature and her spiritual experience in relationship to it is absolutely spirituality. My suggestion was to enhance and learn from those experiences. Each time she encounters that sense of connection and peace when riding, she needs to acknowledge it, savor it, and notice the characteristics of those moments.

I asked Cindy to describe all the qualities necessary to be a successful rider. "Focused yet relaxed; intent but flexible. You need to have firm boundaries regarding what you will let your horse get away with, and a great deal of compassion for them as well. It really doesn't help to be distracted or get too far ahead of yourself. You need to be aware of the moment you are experiencing, without fear. Horses sense fear."

"Wow," I replied, "it sounds like you understand everything you need to about managing stress, and being more spiritual. You have spiritual experiences every time you ride, you just need to apply all that riding wisdom to the rest of your life. If you wrote those qualities down and tried applying them to other areas of your life, I think you'll find the peace you are looking for."

Generally speaking, spiritual experiences are moments that transcend the ordinary mode of perception, meaning, and sensation. Spiritual experiences are typically absorbing; when we are involved in one we aren't thinking about it. When we become self-aware of a spiritual experience it often causes it to change or end. Spiritual experiences are not necessarily of God or religious content, but they do typically give you a sense of relationship to something that defies or transcends the ordinary. Strange as some such experiences may be, they frequently feel as "real" as any ordinary experience of day to day life. Intensity, sensation and emotion are usually altered in a very distinct or dramatic way.

Different types of spiritual experiences, as you will read, have different qualities and manners of seeing and feeling. In some spiritual experiences we have insights about our life path, in others we may encounter sacred beings, and in others we experience a Divine Presence so infinite and self-evident that we are instantly transformed. What matters is that these experiences feel non-ordinary, but teach us and show us things that can change, heal, and improve our relationship to ordinary life.

What Are We Experiencing?

More than simple moments of balance and contentment, spiritual experience can challenge our assumptions about the world and inspire a radically different way of living. In the realms of spiritual experience lie more absurd, profound, divine, and threatening phenomena than you can yet imagine. The Spiritual World is limitless. Experiences of altered or expanded states of consciousness and the Spiritual World can bring us to new perceptions of everyday life, shocking encounters of non-physical beings, subtle energies, and the direct felt-presence of a Divine Source—sometimes with forms and faces, and other times as a pure undifferentiated awareness.

The historical evidence is this: around the world and throughout time, regardless of culture, education, technology or age, people have been having the same styles of spiritual experience. If we look at all the accounts that have been collected, we find they fall into a very simple range. They all converge on common observations and realizations. It is these core experiences that deserve our full attention, whether we feel comfortable with the way they challenge us or not.

For ages spiritual teachers have agreed on two things relating to spiritual experience. The first is that in such experiences we are experiencing "real" things that have substance and an existence of their own. Spiritual experience actually has an objective element. When I guide people in "shamanic journeys," for example, I use sound, breathwork, and visualization to help people access their deepest intuition and open awareness. In these deep states people also encounter experiences of God, Spirit Beings, and deceased ancestors. Consistently, I experience a distinct sensation in my body and in the room *before* people tell me what they are encountering. Sometimes I see what they are seeing, and sometimes they receive my guidance before I speak it. Psychics, mediums, and channels base their careers on consistent "intuitions" about people, places, and things. Gary Schwartz, Ph.D. documented some of these incredible objective elements of spiritual perception and experience in his book *The Afterlife Experiments*.

The second element that spiritual teachers have generally agreed upon throughout time is that true spiritual experiences by their nature *defy* logic and language. That is part of their power and beauty. In shamanic journey work (a form of guided hypnotic imagery exploration) at times I ask the person having the guided imagery experience to narrate what they are experiencing to help them integrate different levels of their awareness. Frequently, people will remain silent though wide awake and clearly engaged. When they do finally speak, they will stammer at a loss for words, simply saying things like, "I can't really put it into words" or "I can't explain it, but it was so real." This is a common hallmark of a spiritual experience.

What Does Science Have to Say?

In recent years there has been a lot of research and debate about the role of the brain, neurology, and psychology in the explanation of spiritual experiences. Currently there are no solid conclusions, only theories. It has been made clear, as in the scientific work of researchers like Rick Hanson, Andrew Newberg, Matthew Alper, and Timothy Jennings that there are regions in the brain specifically associated with spiritual experience, and that we appear to be predisposed to a relationship with higher powers and spiritual forces. Researchers have been able to actually trigger certain kinds of spiritual experience by stimulating specific and targeted regions of the brain. Visions of light, feelings of oneness and the presence of a higher power have all been stimulated in laboratory settings. Neurology is certainly involved in spiritual experience—yet some remain confused by the relationship. Does neurology explain spiritual experience or simply receive and translate it?

It is also no secret that ancient and modern seekers have used psychoactive chemicals, from sacred plants to street drugs, to induce spiritual states of consciousness. This capacity certainly affirms the physical, neurological component, though it does not explain the phenomena. The biochemical and neurological aspect of spiritual experience are sometimes used to suggest that in spiritual experience there is no actual perception of a higher reality, only the abnormal functioning of the brain deluding the observer. This conclusion is poorly reasoned.

While the research shows that human physiology does play a role in spiritual experience. I have no doubt that certain brain structures or distinct forms of neurodivergence can account for people's predisposition to have some types of experiences versus others, and the same conditions may influence frequency. For example, some people have an inborn high absorption and/or dissociation capacity. Dissociation, or disconnecting from present condition thoughts, feelings, or identity, can create real trouble in relationships or in everyday tasks. It can also support the access of spiritual states of consciousness while in meditation, ceremony, yoga, or other practices. Absorption, suggests a tendency to become extremely immersed in sense experiences, or even merged with the world around us. This can be a terrible interruption to a work day, but in the right context this brain-based uniqueness opens us up to spiritual experience.

From "gamma" or flow states, to ADHD and SPS, or Sensory Processing Sensitivity, neurology can help us understand how we access or may be predisposed to spiritual encounters, but in terms of content, meaning, feeling, and inexplicable talents or knowing, neurology and science fall short. For example, the brain can also be stimulated to trigger the smell of burnt toast even when there is no toast present. This does not mean that the next time you smell your toast burning that you should dismiss it as an illusion of the brain, especially if you are making toast at the time or have a teenager fixing their own breakfast. Feelings of love and affection can also be stimulated by a drug or pharmacological agent, but this does not mean that the love you have for your friend, your dog, your child, or your lover is always false or a delusion.

There is no reason to dismiss the opposite possibility, that the brain states can be induced by alternate realities and special forms of subtle energy. Everything we experience, from the most rationally real to the most shockingly sublime is expressed in the brain. Who can clearly say where reality begins: in the perception or in that which is being perceived? The one thing that is clear and agreed upon by scientific and spiritual traditions alike is that the nature of the mind is a mystery.

Science is beginning to understand the brain, but still struggles to understand the "mind." The concept of the "soul" or "spirit" remain deeply contested and resisted by the scientific community, even though most scientists build their careers on spiritual foundations such as intuition, deeply personal motivations, and a sense of inspiration. We all stand upon centuries of stories and evidence of people encountering spiritual beings; dreaming things that come true; and following "hunches" and "vibes" that turn out to be true. Yet to admit such things terrifies many people, religious and scientific alike. The possibility that human awareness can defy time and space upsets all the assumptions we build our lives upon. It demands a new worldview and a new self.

There is a great deal of evidence that has been accumulated in the last one hundred years to affirm and verify that the perceptions in spiritual experience can reveal physical truths of biology, chemistry, and physics. Scientific concepts like "the observer effect"—the power of intention to influence the outcome of experiments—have long been established. Advances in theoretical and quantum physics further affirms notions of subtle fields of energy in all forms of matter, including a unifying field that is within and between all things. Amazingly, astrophysicists have hypothesized that the material world that can be observed comprises less than 5% of our universe. The introduction of ideas like "dark matter" and "dark energy" help account for the remaining 95% of the mass in the universe. This means that even in modern science the vast majority of the known universe can only be understood by inference and theory. This clearly sounds a lot like spiritual truth.

Spiritual principles are congruent with many fields of science. They have long been applied in one of the most conservative sciences: medicine. Placebo, visualization, optimism, and meditation have long been documented as critical factors in health and healing. Visualization, for example, has long been a part of spiritual paths around the world, and many think it is nothing more than imagination. Yet imagined realities have a direct impact on the physical world. For example, modern athletics and medicine have been exploring ways to apply these ancient practices. From martial arts, to football, and competitive weightlifting, studies have shown that athletes that practice and visualize perform better than those who don't. In fact, it has been shown that equal time spent in a combination of visualization and practice produces results equal to the same time of actual performance. Even more incredible, a study regarding muscle strength was also done by the Cleveland Clinic and conclusively showed that visualization alone increased muscle strength.

The results are explained by neurological principles and the fact that the human central nervous system does not differentiate between real and imagined events. This means that spiritual prayers, songs, rituals, readings, contemplations, devotions, and encounters with beings can also have a direct impact on our bodies and our lives. It also means that for some confounding reason, we are "hardwired" to treat the subtle and "imaginative" as seriously as we treat the physical and material world. This science only affirms the importance of spiritual experience.

When people encounter "God's Love," visions of the future, and "Spirit Beings," we are naturally equipped to engage and process it as we would anything else of substance in our lives. The brain is designed to receive and process spiritual experience much the same way it is capable of appreciating music and language.

After working with hundreds, and likely more than one thousand guided imagery clients, I feel confident that intentional and constructed imagery can lead to spontaneous and substantial spiritual experience, independent of any suggestion or plan. Masters and mystics like Ramakrishna taught that the very act of wishing and desperately hoping for spiritual contact and guidance was its own means to summon the very real attention and direction of Spirit. What is called a placebo in science, is often a gateway in spiritual practice: starting with mere intention, effort, and hope, and eventually arriving at something beyond our creation or control.

Why Don't We Know More about Spiritual Experiences?

In traditional cultures the dimensions of spiritual experience and the depth of spiritual practice were typically taught through one of two approaches. First, we find that there was a general education of all community members through mythology and parable. Sacred stories and scriptures are designed to reveal our deepest nature and the power of possibility that we command. In the general community, however, these metaphors and teaching tools are often mistaken for literal truth. Direct experience is reserved for the elite or the ordained, and everyone else is to be content with their reports of The Sacred. Naturally, this is a rule-bound and hierarchical dynamic that easily leads to the *prevention* of spiritual experience. This is common in all cultures.

The second approach focuses on the practical knowledge of the techniques and practices associated with healing and personal power. These "metaphysical" teachings tended to fall under the command of esoteric groups and guilds of healers, teachers, and mystics. Members of specialized or secret societies would have to spend years dedicated to following the practices, protocol, systems, and passages that were set up to ensure the protection of sacred knowledge and experience.

My Lakota spiritual father and mentor, *Wanagi Wachi*, often reminds me of the importance of respecting the spiritual world. "Just because you know the words to a prayer song, or the actions of a ceremony doesn't mean you understand it. The action is only the beginning. In a spiritual practice everything is an act of power, and with that comes responsibility. You have to go slow, approach things with respect, and learn how to protect yourself spiritually. The Spirit World is real and if you don't know what you are doing, you should always ask for help or let someone else do it. It is why we don't take things from other traditions without understanding first. Someone might get hurt."

That Which Is Hidden Must Be Revealed

Because ancient cultures knew that spiritual practices and experiences were at the heart of the power to effect change in the world, they guarded the knowledge of them closely to ensure the safety and order of the community. It is also true that throughout time, sacred practice and experience has been regulated and often controlled through political motives and social class. Even some of the most beautiful mystical paths have been controlled by the upper class or secret societies.

Through my own journey of awakening and healing, I have been invited into the inner circle of many spiritual communities and have come to learn much about the nature of the human spirit and the spiritual world (there were also many groups, practices, and teachings I was *not* allowed to experience). Though there is much that has been trusted to me that I cannot share, there is much that I feel needs to be exposed and passed along—especially in regards to the nature of spiritual experience.

After dramatic and painful years of growing global division and unrest, fueled by political divides, the COVID pandemic, ecological disaster, war, and growing economic disparities, the health of our human communities and the natural world depends on the evolution of consciousness and the awakening of every individual possible. *Your* peace and balance has an impact on much more than your own family and friends. You are a crucial strand in the web of life; your growth and awareness has the power to change the world.

Those of us who have been blessed to enter the inner world of ancient cultures and mystical experiences have the delicate responsibility of educating and co-creating without fostering new forms of cultural appropriation or elitism. Too often, we idolize those who are familiar with the realms of spiritual experience and invite people to hand their wealth and personal power over to them. That is why I feel it is critical to create and share a map of the spiritual world, encouraging you to explore the vehicles by which to travel it. It may assist you on your spiritual journey and empower you to chart a course in which your soul becomes the compass.

Seven Dimensions of the Spiritual World— A Map of The Sacred

So that we don't become lost on our path or in our experiences, it is helpful to have some sense of where it is we have been and where we are going. A map of the sacred will help you to understand what you may encounter, what you may aspire to, and what experiences you must not get attached or addicted to. Each practice and spiritual path is a vehicle that may take us into any number of experiences. These experiences are the terrain that forms a range of predictable territories that span the human experience of God and the Spiritual World. This book will guide you through the landscape of spiritual awakening: a map of spiritual experiences.

It is okay to be attracted to or fascinated by certain types of spiritual experience, but if your goal is true joy, peace, and balance in life, then even amazing and magical states of consciousness can be distractions from a deeper spiritual awakening. Naturally, each person has a tendency toward certain dimensions or territories of the Spiritual World. Often this bias defines our understanding of The Sacred, however it can never represent the true fullness of the spiritual world. The depth of the Spirit is infinite.

There is a common old parable about four wise men (or women) who are sent into a darkened tent to describe what they think is hidden within. Inside is an elephant, but the first wise man reached out and only touched a leg, so he concluded that whatever it is, it is like a tree.

The second wise man grabbed the tail and swore that whatever was in the tent was like a rope. The third found an ear and described it as a sail. The fourth wise man grabbed a tusk and was sure the tent was hiding a weapon of some kind. In fact, none had the complete picture. Until they gathered their experiences together the greater vision could never become clear.

In the same way people become invested in the experience of The Sacred that they have had and resist or reject those that are unfamiliar. Without the collection of experiences to reflect upon, any one vision is incomplete. It helps to be aware of all the common encounters of this Divine Mystery, so we can cultivate a fuller relationship to it, ourselves, and our world.

My goal here is not to create a complicated, perfect new structure that organizes everything spiritual. Nor do I want to propose a solid rational system that argues a particular form of spirituality. There are thousands of models, concepts, and systems for explaining God and the Spiritual World. Endless books and chapters are dedicated to articulating levels of the Spiritual World, the nature of God, and what consciousness is. Our focus is on experience: what is common and what these dimensions *feel* like from the inside out.

Reviewing historical accounts of spiritual experiences and mystical states of consciousness that have been recorded around the world, it is possible to observe basic patterns and themes. Comparing these with the spiritual experiences I have had from childhood to present and contrasting them with the experiences of my clients and colleagues, it is clear that there are seven general and persistent ways we encounter The Sacred. Though it is true that specific religions tend to focus on only one or two of these dimensions while neglecting or denouncing the others, the diversity of experience always shows up in its community members. This partially explains why people in the modern age often seek membership in traditions other than the one they grew up in. They are attracted to the practices and philosophies that match their spiritual experience, not their heritage. They long for something that matches their inner world, not their outer world.

It is also worth noting the growing contemporary interest in psychedelics and psychoactive natural medicines. Mind-altering medicines are being used more and more in a wide range of settings from sacred personal ceremonies of self-exploration, to outdoor concerts, group retreats, psychological therapy, cancer treatment, and even in some workplaces for performance enhancement. While I have intentionally made the decision not to uplift psychedelics as a mechanism or pathway for spiritual experience in this book, the experiences that people have while under the influence of "mind-altering" medicines, sacraments, and recreational drugs certainly also fall within the seven categories of experience mapped herein.

Traditional cultures around the world, including the roots of the major "world religions" all show some use of consciousness-altering medicines and/or behaviors. The significance is simple: if spiritual experiences didn't matter these practices and plants would have been abandoned centuries ago. I am neither for nor against psychedelics, but want to assure each reader that every type of spiritual experience on our map has been accessed at one point or another by every and any type of spiritual practice. I have chosen to write exclusively about experiences that have not been influenced by any medicine or drug, and in some cases were virtually spontaneous.

As I explain in detail in the book *Return to the Sacred*, spiritual practices persist around the world and throughout time because they have an effect that is meaningful. The path you choose to open your heart and relax your mind must be chosen with care and ideally guided by someone with experience, expertise, and knowledge of your risks, goals, and liabilities. Nevertheless, while there is no shortage of recommended spiritual practices, a clear understanding of where they may take you, what it all means, and how it is all interrelated is typically an afterthought.

My goal in this book is simply to help you to recognize the common ways people encounter The Sacred—God, consciousness and the Spiritual World—so that you can recognize when you are having such an encounter and make the most of it. Each "way" of encountering The Sacred leads us to a different set of assumptions about spirituality, Spiritual Beings, God, ourselves and the world. Knowing the seven different ways people experience The Sacred helps us to have a bigger context to understand our unique journey as individuals. Each type of spiritual experience provides a different lens on who and what we are, as well as a unified validation of the expansive and transcendent nature of consciousness. Ultimately, you may come to see spiritual experience just as the mystics throughout the ages have: as many expressions of the One Sacred Source. All as One, all is One. This is what I refer to as "The Sacred."

The seven ways we experience The Sacred can be titled:

1. The Experience of Truth and Beauty
2. The Experience of Ordinary Magic
3. The Experience of the Spirit World
4. The Experience of the Cosmic Self
5. The Experience of Divine Energy
6. The Experience of the Formless Spirit
7. The Experience of Pure Consciousness

These seven experiences are ordered in a hierarchy of integration. Each experience assists us to make sense of the level that precedes it, but each experience cannot fully understand the view that follows it. Level 2 helps us understand level 1, but not level 3. Level 4 helps us understand levels 1, 2, 3, but not level 6. For example, once we have had an experience of the "Cosmic Self," it is possible to understand and integrate the experiences we have of the "Spirit World." But, if we have only experienced the "Spirit World" then we may not yet understand the experience of the "Cosmic Self." This distinction will become clear and obvious later. It is helpful to know, but not important at this point. In some cases, an experience of a type of spiritual encounter can be so distinct and state-dependent that it may not feel like any other type of spiritual experience can or does exist. This is a central problem for religious groups of the world who often pursue only one variety of experience and use it alone to validate their story of reality and meaning.

I encourage you to be contemplative—reflective, open-minded, and intuitive—as you explore and develop new spiritual experiences in your own life. Your own research and considerations will help you to expand and build your own sense of the universe, its order, and your place in it. Ultimately, mystery stands out as one of the persistent hallmarks of our world—material and spiritual. A willingness to explore with sincerity and open-mindedness will reveal most of what you seek.

The numbered ordering of the seven reflects their relationships, *but not their value*. All are significant, all have the power to heal and help. All types of spiritual experience are meaningful if we learn from them. The ideal way to think of these categories of experiences is on a continuum, in a circle, for as we go to the furthest extreme, we find a connection with the very beginning level. Hierarchies appeal too much to the ego, and it is easy to become spiritually competitive or self-important.

Many modern spiritual seekers assume the most exotic experiences are the best. Exotic and rare spiritual experiences are important because of what they teach, but they are not of greater worth or value than any other experience. When experiences, practices, time-tested teachers, and living communities are isolated from one another it becomes natural to judge what is unfamiliar. When seekers and spiritual leaders are not in dialogue with each other and the wider world then we begin to feel that some ways are right and some are wrong. If we have an isolated view of spiritual experience, attachment and judgement begin to grow and the path of peace is cut short. Collectively, all spiritual experiences are necessary to our most profound relationships to the Ultimate Nature of Being. All spiritual experiences contribute to the richness of the world community.

What matters is what makes a difference. If a person only experiences one of these domains, and yet becomes fully self-actualized, compassionately connected and "deeply awakened" then there is no need for the pursuit or envy of the others. The realization of the true nature of our selves and The Sacred can come to anyone, at any time, and unfolds differently for each of us. That is part of the beauty of the human journey.

Now, relax your mind, open your heart and let's proceed into The Sacred.

Chapter Two

The Experience of Truth and Beauty

When the soul connects with a reflection of itself,
or a glimpse of the greater Spirit
in the elegant designs of life,
peace, vitality, and joy rise to the surface.
That is why the experience of Truth and Beauty gives hope.
It teaches us to embrace each moment and to discover the depth
of who we truly are.

Home Away from Home

It had been a hot South African day. The sun sank towards the horizon, casting an orange glow and deep shadows across the land. The old pickup sped down the dirt road through small villages, fields, and pastures. I was entranced by the changing landscapes and the passing villages. My mind was intoxicated by the world of endless stories growing from the rich red earth, the distant mountains and simple yet lush green fields.

My dear Venda brother, Sammy, and I pulled into the small cluster of clay buildings, and made our way to the small central courtyard. The low buildings were simple and worn. The courtyard was filled with old chairs and weathered benches. *Mokomana* (my elder brother) Sammy introduced me to a few people and we found our way to a seat, amongst the gathering crowd. I was among the Lemba for the first time.

This amazing group of people identify themselves as "the black Jews" and many believe themselves to be direct descendants of one of the original 12 tribes of Israel. The Lemba migrated south through Africa to where they now live in South Africa and Zimbabwe. Researchers suggest there is evidence for common DNA shared between certain ancient Jewish bloodlines and the Lemba.

It is, however, only a small number of traditions and some religious objects and garments, that are common to both Jews and Lemba today. The Lemba are much more Christian and African in their traditions than anything else. Nevertheless, my African family thought that as a Jew it would be interesting for me to attend one of their services, and I agreed.

By the time everyone assembled in the rows of seats in the courtyard, the sun had set and the sky was slowly turning into a deep lavender sea. The beauty, the novelty, and the anticipation pulled me further into the moment. Thoughts of home, expectations, and ideas slowly disappeared. The minister stepped forward from the dark row of shadowed chairs that were lined up behind the altar, and began with passionate words in the Lemba language. The people nodded heads, and made sounds of affirmation.

Another man stood up from the dark and the two broke into song. In an instant the entire community joined, as if on cue, and I felt myself engulfed by the rich harmonies and the swelling melody. The hair stood up on my arms, and I felt a flood of emotion. I did not understand anything that was being said or done, but I could feel the sincerity and love with which these people prayed and I thought my heart was going to burst as it swelled with the overwhelming majesty of this beauty and raw spirit. I was caught up in a flood of emotion.

The service continued. Experiencing the flow of energy between the pastors and the congregation was like witnessing the intimate life of a couple. There was passion, and intensity, there was anger and surrender, there was hope, joy, and always, always, creation in harmony. The harmony of voice, and heart and soul was so astounding, I could only release my mind's desire to discern what each movement meant, and I simply fell into the depth of the spirit.

At that very moment, a giant moon exposed itself, floating up over the roof of the building behind the preachers, who were now almost impossible to see in the dark evening shadows. At times I could see their animated expressions when they stepped forward into the light of the candle that was placed on the simple wooden altar. I was transfixed by the enormous shining silver disc in the sky.

Life in that moment was as sweet and as precious as I could imagine. The pure bliss within that moment was all I could grasp, and I felt at home, here in this place so strange and new. Beyond the facades of culture, distance, and language; there was the universal beauty of human spirit. I experienced it as a quality of grace pouring out over each and every one of us. A humble collection of souls united in the love of something greater and the desire to make a better life and to find peace. There were no words for the truth and beauty of that moment.

When the heart is truly open and awake, there is no difference between prayers or feelings or songs to God. When the heart is truly listening, language does not matter. Where there is a sincere desire to connect to The Sacred directly, to truly merge with the awareness of the Sacred Energy of Life, there people become as one mind. In that moment, the "right" belief or religious practice is irrelevant. The presence of something Sacred transcends all. The true longing heart for God knows no culture, no history, no politics. It does not require religion or to be right, only the ability to be fully present and so to see the world as it truly is.

What Is the Experience of Truth and Beauty?

Moments such as this one are most memorable when they happen in unusual places, at momentous times, or with people who are special to us. My favorite way to work with groups is in the incredible and beautiful embrace of far-off places and meaningful travel. When I lead retreat groups to Southern Africa it is the power of the place, the people, the culture, and the wildlife that awaken people's sense of Spirit and a renewed passion for life. But, in actuality, I do little to "make" such things happen. Life is the Master Teacher. These powerful "ah-ha" moments shine in the light of the exotic, but the actual energy, feeling, and insight is available all the time and everywhere. Such moments are happening all the time, and all around us. Impatience, boredom, routine, worry, fear, doubt, and stress are examples of the many daily moods that blind us from the brilliance of life. Now more than ever, pure distraction and the obsession with digital entertainment, from social media to streaming content, means the mind is less and less ripe for these special moments. Yet, they are always close at hand.

There are many things that create moments of truth and beauty: a good laugh, an old friend, an amazing meal, a work of art, laying in the grass, getting lost in a game of basketball or golf, even the colors and rhythms of a busy city street. In these common blissful experiences, it is typically not the circumstance that makes the situation so incredible, it is the way you are seeing it. It is the fact that in that moment you aren't thinking of any other moment. You are fully present.

It is natural for people to be more fully present under some conditions than in others, yet the secret remains, beauty is in the eye of the beholder. The famous French author and philosopher Marcel Proust was noted for observing, "The voyage of discovery is not in seeking new landscapes but in having new eyes." So it is in moments of Truth and Beauty—we have new eyes for something ordinary. The tangible turns us to a feeling greater than we can explain.

What we learn from these moments is that happiness is a spiritual experience. Why? It occurs most vibrantly when we are free of our ego-driven consciousness, and in deep relationship with what makes us unique. The idea of the "true self" becomes more apparent in such moments. If you pay attention, they will teach you where you find vitality, meaning, and connection. Simple and mundane as they may seem, moments of Truth and Beauty are what most of us live for; still we often fail to see how they are but the first steps of the path to understanding The Sacred. In these experiences we learn the power of the moment and are being given the greatest clue to the secret of life that the great mystics have taught for ages: everyday life is sacred.

In experiences of Truth and Beauty we become absorbed in the present moment. We could be eating cherries, going for a walk, or observing the beauty of a person or place. In such a moment we don't transcend the world, rather we become deeply and fully engaged *in* the world. The challenge for most of us is that we allow such moments to occur based on preferences, desire, or comfort. If only we would extend that same love and appreciation to all things, then we might find a new experience of the world: wisdom in wounding, friends in enemies, lessons and love hiding everywhere we go.

I was reminded of this recently when I ran into an old client. This man is not one of my favorite people to be around. He talks without stopping, has little regard for my time, constantly promotes himself and his own spiritual "powers" and never pays much attention to his influence or impact on others (unless it's a positive one). Frequently, he is also rude and speaks in a way that many people find insulting. When I saw Barry it was an experience like all the previous ones. I felt my mind wander; I was noticing people passing on the street behind him. I was trying not to look at my watch too much. Suddenly, I became aware of my resistance to the moment I was in.

I realized that because he was a client and a good patron of the place I worked, I decided I was not about to abruptly end my conversation to escape. Having consciously made this first choice, it occurred to me that the next choice I had was to be *in* the moment I had chosen. I wondered how I could connect with the Truth and Beauty of the moment?

I asked myself, how would his mother or lover look upon him? What do the people who like him see? What do the people who he helps feel about him? What if I opened my heart to him—more—not less? What if I was fully present? Presence is a practice that can transform any moment.

Listening earnestly and gazing with growing affection I began to appreciate Barry like a work of art. His annoying qualities became comical, and his gifts and wisdom became apparent. I found myself really listening and seeing beneath the surface. Behind his breathless words was simply the desire to be liked and appreciated. He was no different than most people at that level. In fact, I also learned something about myself and how I resist "letting myself" be as free and unchecked, and it is likely that created a sense of unnamed resentment.

Then, something amazing happened. As if he finally felt "heard" for the first time since I knew him, Barry initiated the end of our conversation! It was as if by being fully present, we both got what we needed from the conversation, and let go of the pieces that divided us. Typically I would have been caught up in judgment and distraction. Looking for Truth and Beauty changed everything.

When and Where?

Experiences of Truth and Beauty are often thought of as peak experiences, "a-ha" moments, or the freedom from life's burdens: "a moment of peace." Though we have the power to choose the mindset that evokes an experience of Truth and Beauty, these experiences may spontaneously occur in almost any setting. For those who still struggle to think of personal examples, it is helpful to know that the experience of Truth and Beauty commonly occurs:

- In nature
- During deep relaxation
- On vacation
- In moments of intimacy
- In the presence of remarkable art or science
- During surprises
- During sexual and sensual moments
- At the completion of a significant process or journey
- Graduation, completing a test, or after a first successful performance
- When fear is overcome
- In the complete absence of stress
- When you are fully present
- When critical choices become suddenly clear
- During an important and transformative insight
- Playing a sport or instrument you love and feel accomplished at.

Sometimes When You Least Expect It

One woman, Barbara, told me the story of her struggle with grief and loss after her husband of 42 years had died. She talked about how inconsolable she was; nothing seemed to help: no therapy, bereavement groups, talking with family, or retreating on her own. One day Barbara was traveling to visit family on the west coast. She spent the day driving and had an overnight on the way.

The drive, she recalled, was terrible. She felt sad and lonely, remembering how much she used to love road trips with her husband. In the late evening, after dark, she pulled into a roadside hotel in a small tourist town. Barbara suspected that she was nearing a wilderness area, but was too tired and preoccupied to bother to ask about her whereabouts when she checked into the hotel. Once she made it to her room, she was struck with grief. Another empty room, another place alone, another reminder of her loss. It began to rain and she fell into a restless sleep. Filled with worry about her future, and shame about how poorly she was handling her situation, she hardly slept a solid hour through the night.

Finally, the first sounds of morning were outside her window and Barbara decided to go for a walk. She thought that some fresh air might calm her down and help her to be alert for her last day of driving. "There was a road out behind the hotel, and a sign that said something about a lake or a pond," she recollected.

"I was cold at first, and could not see much. As I walked, the sky began to lighten up and I could smell the earth still wet from the rain. Finally, I came to the lake. It really was more of a pond, a large duck pond. I watched the water birds come and go. Some fished for breakfast, some were in pairs, some were alone and some swam in groups. I am not sure what caught my attention, but for a moment I wasn't thinking anything at all, I was just in a trance." Barbara acted surprised as she recalled this.

"Maybe I was so tired. Tired of being sad and tired. Maybe it was watching the simplicity of the ducks going about their morning routine. It was so peaceful. There was obvious challenge, hardship, and uncertainty but they were fully present with the tasks at hand. I'll never know, but they don't seem to suffer the mind's effects as we do. It gave me a sense of permission.

"I found myself letting go of the memories that haunted me, and releasing the constant worry of the future. Something about that place held my attention. All of a sudden, I looked up, and right there the very top of the sun was cresting over the horizon in the east. Suddenly I realized that there was an incredible world wrapped around me. Not too far away I could see a small town, ranches and fields, patches of wilderness, and the highway stretching into the distance. It's very hard to describe, but in that moment, the beauty pulled me out of my sorrow.

"I realized that I had been lost in myself. Lost in my feelings, just like that amazing morning, the way I began my day—surrounded by beauty, yet totally unaware of it. I was unaware that the world was going on without me. And, you know, it is not such a bad place. I was always looking for what reminded me of what I lost, and instead, I was suddenly reminded of what was yet to find!

"In that moment, I knew I'd be okay. I knew I'd get through and that it is what my husband would have wanted. No one was there to tell me any of this, but it was real to me, as real as anything. My terrible journey got easier and easier from that day on. I would say that I've learned a lot since then. Maybe, I've never been so aware of my life."

Barbara's story is not uncommon. People have shared stories with me about their darkest days and the way one moment, one sight, one sound, one person's outstretched hand, turned it all around. Truth and beauty do not always come in the same way nor are they both always obvious.

Sometimes the truth is revealed later, sometimes the beauty is felt looking back. These moments reveal a hidden wisdom in the world and in ourselves.

***

Recently I worked with a person who once had a heroin addiction. I asked, "How were you ever able to quit?" She replied, lightly, "I did it on my own. I pretty much locked myself in my house until it fought its way out of me." She laughed. "You know, I was out with my friends one day, we were getting high in the back of a night club. I looked around and all of a sudden, I saw everything. I mean I *saw* the situation clearly—as if it was a movie—and it was awful. It was ugly and sick. We weren't glamorous, we weren't having fun, we were just deprived, lonely, lost. We were looking for a moment of truth or bliss, but really we were escaping life. I could see my life clearly, maybe for the first time. It was a total moment of truth, and I knew I had to change or I would die. That weekend I quit heroin, cocaine, all that stuff. It was one of the hardest things to do, but that moment was so clear. I just had to make a choice."

Everyone and Anyone

Athletes, artists, scientists, parents and children, rich and poor, sick and well, all people may have such moments of Truth and Beauty. These are moments when something within us finally sees the world, a situation or ourselves clearly; a beauty is revealed that we normally miss. We encounter what feels like the absolute truth and it can motivate us to make powerful changes if we pay attention and observe what we are being shown.

These moments of clarity come at surprising times, and often when we need it most. What we experience is more than psychology or motivation. It is an awareness that is hard to describe, but easy to recognize for most of us. For most people, the challenge is not learning how to have the experience, it is learning to acknowledge and learn from it. The challenge is remembering that it showed us that appreciation, gratitude, love, and peace are all possible.

Sadly, many people use such moments to escape life, rather than embrace it. Sex, shopping, money, power, recreation, and relaxation all become about avoiding life. I think of professional athletes as an interesting example. The most important aspect of an athlete's performance is not their performance, it is how they use their time off. Most elite athletes spend the off season practicing, training, and preparing for peak performance.

Imagine if the only time Tiger Woods played golf was when he was in a tournament. Imagine if the only time Michael Jordan played basketball was when he had a game. It makes no sense. Day to day life is like a championship game. If you see your joys and pleasures as an "escape" or as disconnected from the rest of your life, you will always struggle to experience a deeper level of peace in daily life. If you recognize that the moments you love the most are teaching you how to handle the moments you love the least, you will win the game every time.

The idea that life is divided into categories that do not touch each other is false. It may be easy to think of work, rest, play, family, friends, obligations, and choices as separate events and compartments of your life. But they are all a part of one single journey: yours. Every moment expresses and offers a choice. Each aspect of life can help or hinder the other. Embrace the presence of Truth and Beauty in your life and let it grow in your awareness. Let it shape your choices and intentions.

****

I recall Greg who came to see me because he was frustrated by the way his work and family routines had come to consume him. He felt lost and as if he could not even imagine what "being spiritual" could be like, although he was sure it was something he wanted in his life. I had encouraged him to attend an afternoon workshop I was running about spiritual experiences and the great mystical teachings.

At one point in the workshop, I asked people to share a story of one experience they have had of "Truth and Beauty." They could share any simple or profound story of an ordinary moment that became extraordinary. The small group proceeded and one after another people shared stories about where and when they have had such Sacred moments: young love in high school; overcoming an abusive relationship; watching the moon rise over a city; the moment they knew they'd survive a terrible divorce; the recognition of their power to break a family cycle of violence; running into an old friend in a far off country; sitting at the edge of the Grand Canyon.

As it drew near to Greg's turn he became visibly uncomfortable. Finally, it was his turn and he sat in silence. "I just don't think I have ever had an experience like what you guys are talking about. I'm a pretty simple guy. I haven't traveled much. I don't get out in nature much either."

I encouraged him to think of times where he felt a sense of peace or freedom: no worries, no stress, just fully present and maybe even surprised. "How about at a baseball game?" he joked. "Maybe," I answered and asked him to say more.

"Well, for me, I don't go often, but when I do, it's magical. Seriously. Once that game begins, it's like there is nothing in the world but the field, the players, the lights, the crowd. Slowly, my attention draws in, and I *am in the game*. I feel like I am sitting on the base coach's shoulder. I feel like I can see through the pitcher's eyes. I feel this thrill with every point and agony with every defeat. It's silly I guess. But when I watch baseball, something inside me relaxes and something else in me seems to fly. I can feel the whole stadium inside me. I *am* the players on the field.

Now, is that weird? I told you I don't have any spiritual stories."

We all sat in silence. His words had been so poetic, his feelings so strong. Everyone knew that he was describing exactly the kind of sacred moments they had talked about. Still, he didn't see it for himself. I asked Greg, "If you could describe the qualities of your experience, without using the actual events of baseball, what qualities would you list?" I went to a board to write his words down for all to see.

"Well," he began slowly, "Focused. Totally present. Peaceful. Calm and excited. Connected to everything around me. Alive! Really alive! Ten feet tall! Happy." There was enthusiasm in his voice. Everyone smiled. He looked at his list. "Wow. I guess that does sound pretty spiritual. Sounds like church! Heck, I only wish I felt like that in church!"

Everyone laughed warmly with him. "Yes," I added, "for you, that is like going to church. If you take the time to think about it, take the time to reflect on it, there are probably other times like that in your life. You can seek them, nurture them, feed them."

The Lessons

A moment of Truth and Beauty may be simple and fleeting, but strung together, like pearls, we begin to become aware of a radiant dimension to life. When people say "stop and smell the roses" or "it's the little things that count" they are referring to the growing awareness that no matter how difficult things become there is always a feeling of connection, hope, and benevolence lurking in the shadows.

Truth and Beauty give us the gift of hope and the taste of happiness. In such experiences we realize that whenever we can be fully present we find a taste of peace that confirms for us that things will work out. When we experience Truth and Beauty we are fully present, it teaches us to not be caught up in the past, the future, or stories in our minds. Experiences of Truth and Beauty reveal the senses of the soul.

Such times show our true passions, the things that help us to feel connected and what is most important. Though easily dismissed in the search for more dramatic highs, the experience of Truth and Beauty is critical to knowing who we are as a unique soul in this world. Pay attention to those experiences and you will find the essential keys to fulfilment, meaning, and vitality that are distinct and essential to you alone.

Such times are also the evidence of the power of being attentive to the moment we are in.

This is like the call of the Spirit. We need no medical research or Zen master to teach us why "being in the moment" is healing. If you think of a moment of Truth and Beauty, you know for yourself that releasing the obsession with analysis of the past and constant desires to control the future are exactly what create the stress and imbalance you seek to end. If you cultivate the heart's passions, and the mind's ability to attend to what is occurring right now, you will quickly be on the road to personal peace.

When we encounter Truth and Beauty in a way that resonates within, we are no longer seeing with the eyes of our persona—our ego and social self. Instead, we are seeing beyond all the "shoulds" and "expectations." The eyes of the soul always sense what feels right, what is authentic and honoring of our deepest needs. When the soul connects with a reflection of itself, peace, vitality and joy rise to the surface. That is why the experience of Truth and Beauty gives hope, teaches us to embrace each moment and discover who we truly are.

Exercise

Sit down and make a list of people, situations, and places where you have felt a deep sense of peace, contentment, happiness, and/or connection. Place a star beside the ones you can recreate or revisit on a regular basis. Then, write a list of:

1. The qualities and feelings you experienced in those moments
2. The other situations in life in which you'd like to see those same qualities
3. The excuses or reasons you create for why you do not spend more time doing the things that you placed a star beside.

Finally, pick two of the items you marked as repeatable and create a simple plan for how you will reintegrate them into your life on a regular basis for a period of 90 days. Remember to be specific and decide when you will begin, and who you will ask to support you.

Chapter Three

The Experience of Ordinary Magic

More than healing powers, special talents, or power over events,
the real gift of Ordinary Magic is the cultivation
of a sense of wonder, curiosity, open-mindedness, and possibility.
It is the knowledge that this world is full
of more possibilities and more mysterious than you will ever know.

Entering the Magic

It was late evening, and I was sitting in the basement of a small Indigenous American reservation home in Pine Ridge, South Dakota, the land of the Lakota, Sioux. It was a fairly large rectangular room, windowless, without furniture. Around the perimeter of the room community members sat against the wall on pillows and blankets. I was the only non-local I could detect.

The room was dimly lit and people were talking and joking quietly, waiting for the ceremony to begin. These were people who came seeking healing, connection, blessing, and with a desire to support those who came for help with their prayers. In the middle of the room, a blanket was laid out. On it was an elaborate and intricate arrangement of ceremonial objects.

The *Wapiye*, the healer, was busy preparing the ritual items and himself. He seemed to be slowing down his movements with each moment. It seemed as if his actions were becoming more precise, more contemplative with each passing second. This man, whom anthropologists would call a "shaman," was well recognized throughout the surrounding areas for his amazing abilities to heal through a special ceremony known as the *Yuwipi*. The *Yuwipi* is a ceremony in which the healer communicates with the spiritual world—sacred forces and spiritual beings—to assist in the helping and healing of individuals and the community.

At one side of the room, his assistants and the ceremonial drummers prepared themselves. His lead assistant moved about the room organizing people and protocol. I was sitting in a sort of "honor seat," the seat at the head of the room. This was the seat for the person who called for the ceremony, the main sponsor who asked for healing. That was me. I had never experienced anything like this before. I didn't know anyone in the room and I was the only non-native person present. I had no idea what to expect and was filled with a mixture of emotions: excitement, anxiety, fear, uncertainty, and a strange undercurrent of peace. Years ago when my problem first began I would have never expected that this is where it would lead me.

When I was an infant the doctors noticed that I was pigeon-toed and wanted to "correct" the "problem" with leg braces. They were sure this course of action was to prevent me from future problems. Until the age of thirteen I had no obvious problems or pains in my feet and legs. I enjoyed an active childhood. At the age of thirteen, however, I developed a problem in my feet and legs.

I experienced sharp pain in my knees and hips when running, or walking long distances. I continued to play sports and began to sprain my ankles repeatedly. Soon I was forced to withdraw from many of the high-intensity physical activity programs in my high school. Ultimately, it turns out that when I was a child the problem was over-corrected, and my legs were turned outward causing a misalignment of my ankles, knees and hips.

Over the years of high school my parents pursued many options and all the specialists we could track down. The choices were always few: prosthetics, surgery, physiotherapy. The most significant option was to "break" my feet and then reconstruct them to include an arch and realign my legs. That did not feel like a reasonable intervention, and so I decreased my physical activity, focused on my spiritual pursuits and hoped that one day I'd meet a healer who could help. Years later, after I had begun to journey in the world of Indigenous American spirituality and tradition, I asked my Lakota mentor and spiritual father, *Wanagi Wachi* if he knew of any medicine in his culture that could help. That is how I ended up in that far-off place.

The time for the ceremony to begin was drawing near. I was feeling isolated and unsure. I had never experienced anything like this before and had no idea what to expect. I was torn between my disbelief and my desire for healing. I wanted to believe that somehow this healer could work some magic and change my body, but everything I knew told me otherwise.

Just then, the lead assistant to the healer approached me. He kneeled closely and looked at me intensely. "I don't care where you are from or what you believe. Tonight we all need to be of one mind for this healing to work and so no one gets hurt. This is no time for fear or doubt. You asked for this and now a lot of people are here to support you and to ask for their own healing. For some people here, this night means more than you can imagine."

"This man," he motioned toward the healer, "he is risking his life for you. As long as this ceremony goes on, you focus on your prayers, positive thoughts and trust that this will work. Do that and everything will be fine." He left as abruptly as he came. Everyone suddenly settled down. He took his seat. The healer moved to the middle of the room, sat on the altar space in the middle of the room, and the lights were turned out. I was at a total loss, not knowing what to expect, what to do, or even how to relate to what was happening. Excited, scared, trying to keep an open mind and willing heart, the setting became overwhelming and something in me pulled my awareness into the dark silence and I simply waited.

The drums began, then the singing began. The room had been prepared so that not the slightest bit of light could enter. It was pitch black. I heard songs and sounds I'd never heard before, I felt an excitement and a nervousness that was hard to contain. My mind raced to make sense of what was happening. But there was nothing familiar to grasp. At first I heard the healer praying in his language, Lakota: the tones and words were strange to me, but beautiful, powerful and comforting. Soon after, the healer fell silent. The ceremony, drumming, and singing continued for hours.

Deep into the ceremony I heard the sound of a rattle shaking in the middle of the room. I looked into the darkness to see if there was a sign of movement. I couldn't see anything—not my hand in front of my face. Then, a flash. I saw flashes of blue light dancing around where the healer had sat. I had read about Spirits appearing in ceremonies as blue lights, but never thought it to be literally true. Then the rattle began to glow. It flickered on and off, then faded to black again.

The next thing I knew the rattle was right in front of me. As if it had flown from the healer's hand to me. I sensed he was there before me as well. I could not imagine how he moved from the complex arrangement of objects without knocking things over, nor could I imagine how he located me precisely in the absolutely blacked-out room.

The rattle immediately went to my body, as if attracted to the exact places I had experienced pain. It did not fumble or search, it was exact, touching me lightly, but vigorously. Then the light began to flash again. I could tell what it was, but I felt like crying. Tears welled up. Emotion surged. I wasn't scared or sad, but felt blessed. I felt the most profound gratitude. I didn't understand any of it, but somehow I felt that something, or someone was present to help.

Somehow it seemed that the world was much, much greater than anything I imagined. The rattle then moved. It danced around the room and stopped in specific places on specific people. It seemed that it was the tool of healing. This continued for some time. I prayed and prayed for everyone in the room. I prayed for my healer and for myself. I prayed for all I didn't understand and gave thanks to whatever was present.

When it was over and lights came on, I was relieved and yet sad that the dark cocoon of ceremony was dissolving. People began to talk again. A few rituals followed and late into the night the whole event was brought to a close. At that time the healer called me over to him. He shook my hand. "You'll be fine," he said with quiet confidence. "Here, take this." It was a piece of a root as wide as two fingers, but no longer than my thumb.

"Every day you can grate some of this into a powder. Make two cups of tea with it. Drink one cup and use the other to wash the parts that trouble you. Make sure you pray as you do these things." I looked at the small root and worried it was not enough. I wondered how a simple tea could change the structure of my bones, muscles, and eliminate the pain I was so used to. "Could I have a little more?" I asked. He laughed and smiled. "You take this until it works. If you run out, give me a call, I'll mail you more."

It was only six weeks later that I stopped taking the medicine. I got rid of my whole-foot prosthetics. I started exercising, hiking, and running again and have never had trouble since. I still have half of that root today. I cannot explain why or how that ceremony worked, but it healed my body, changed my life, and I remember every day, with each step I take, that true magic is not only possible—it is more common than we think.

What Is Ordinary Magic?

At the time I experienced that healing ceremony I did not understand, as I do now, the techniques, factors, and elements that went into its success—not that I can understand anything fully now or ever. Not understanding "how" did not prevent me from experiencing amazement and empowerment from the success of the ritual. Looking back, nearly 30 years later, I have seen many such "miracles"—not only among Indigenous healers, but in the lives of the people I meet day to day. Often, conversations about spirituality evoke a reflection on the mysterious and amazing moments of life: the experiences of Ordinary Magic.

In experiences of Ordinary Magic we spontaneously encounter events and experiences that defy the common laws of nature. At the simplest level, it might be in an intuition that comes true, or an unexplainable synchronicity, or even the personal witness of the surprising capacities of the human mind, body, or sensory system. More extreme examples include miracles, unexplainable phenomena, and experiences of mystery that heal and uplift. In experiences of Ordinary Magic we may directly experience our capacity to connect with information in a way that defies time and space. When I share the story of how I was physically healed by a ceremony I discover that many people have an experience of Ordinary Magic. It excites and inspires—even though it is not their story. Direct and indirect experiences of miracles of the body, unexplainable changes in health, healing, and the power of thought and feeling are all a part of Ordinary Magic. In these experiences, we may access information that comes from distant times and places, perceive subtle forms of energy and sound, or experience stories and evidence of how these capacities can help and heal. In such experiences we are not yet masters of these surprising realities, but the connection to them has a profound impact.

Having grown up in a typical North American home, we did not speak of spirits, miracles, or the power of the mind to create radical changes in the world. We did learn about the influence of attitude, and there was always a very humanistic openness to respect the rights and claims of others, regardless of what it was about. It has taken me time and a great deal of experience to overcome my own skepticism about Ordinary Magic. Nevertheless, I have come to refer to these moments as Ordinary Magic for I have come to see that they are both inexplicable and commonplace—more than most would care to admit. In fact, I have come to see how simple it is (though not always easy) to co-create acts of Ordinary Magic to help heal and navigate life's challenges and opportunities.

Thinking back, I grew up with friends whose ability to consider the improbable was further compromised by fear. I recall a conversation about spiritual practices like meditation and yoga with a friend of mine when we were teenagers. Neither of us had tried any such thing, but we were speculating that they sounded like something worth trying. For me, the conversation was only a matter of exploring something unfamiliar, for my friend it was much more complicated. "You don't understand," he said in frustration, "you never grew up with the fear of hell. I did. If this is the wrong thing, if God doesn't like me doing these things, I have to deal with the worst fate you can imagine." Fortunately, I hadn't imagined a horrible fate and the exploration was simple for me. For my friend, his fear was paralyzing.

The story parallels the big obstacle to experiences of Ordinary Magic: the willingness to consider the impossible and unfamiliar. Later in life

I experienced a similarly telling moment about human nature. I was working as the director of Spiritual Care Services in a university affiliated hospital in Canada. I had just established a staff wellness program based on volunteer alternative and complementary healers offering treatments for staff.

Soon after we launched the program the vice-president of nursing, my boss, received a letter of outrage from a hospital geneticist, Dr. Carl. Hearing that "energy healers" and people who practice complementary medicine were on the property was an absolute insult. His objection to energy medicine being used to heal patients and staff was so extreme he threatened to quit if it was not stopped.

My wonderful boss helped to explain to him that the healers were not coming to see patients, and that the only service being offered to staff was "relaxation," not healing. He relented and withdrew his complaint. I was asked to meet with him to answer questions that he might have and to assure him that what he was told would be true. Our meeting was a pivotal moment for me.

"I'll let you know right off the bat, that there is no evidence to support the idea that spiritual healing, or energy healing does anything at all. It is a lot of wishful thinking, just like the rest of spirituality. I believe in evidence. It's quite simple." Dr. Carl's opening comments were very firm and almost attacking.

"Have you ever experienced any of the energy medicines like acupuncture, reiki, therapeutic touch, or healing touch?"

"No."

"Well, I don't blame you," I said. "I really didn't believe these things either—until I experienced them. Then I started to look up the research and found that there is evidence to support their effectiveness." I was sincerely sympathetic.

"You really believe that? People can do research to suit their needs you know," he responded.

"True, however that comment really doesn't support the evidence you have *against* these things, any more than it casts doubt on the evidence for these things. I'd love to show you the research I have compiled and then you can look at it yourself. You have more experience in scientific review than I do. Maybe you can see the flaw or the truth in the data." I was willing to let the science speak for itself.

"What makes you believe healing through nothing more than the energy of a person's hands and their intentions can make a difference?" he asked. Dr. Carl's tone was softening and becoming more curious.

Not mentioning the healing ceremony that had been done for my feet, I began by describing that many things I once thought impossible I had since learned to be true. "It is not uncommon for me to dream something that will either come true or give me information about something in my life."

He laughed a bit, "That's just a self-fulfilling prophecy. You see yourself doing something, so then you do it."

Curiously and conveniently, I had an unusual series of recent examples to give him that all involved owls. "Over the last year," I shared, "whenever I dream of an owl, the next day I see one. It hasn't happened too often, but often enough–maybe four times. Each time was more surprising than the previous. Only a few weeks ago I dreamt of a white owl. I awoke and told someone of the dream. They asked me what the owl represented. I said, 'I think it means I am going to see a white owl. No symbolism.' The next day, with a witness in the car, in early September, right in the middle of the road I was driving on, the person I was driving with, and I, saw a white owl."

I will never forget his response. "It is not really significant unless you write it down. How do I know you aren't twisting the facts?"

My desire to convince Dr. Carl of the existence of Ordinary Magic was quickly dissolving.

We talked a bit longer about matters at the hospital, and about his children and some of his interests. As we finished our lunch meeting, he offered, "We can meet again if you want to show me that research." I was surprised, but willing.

A couple of weeks later I set up another meeting with Dr. Carl. Our first exchange had ended on a pleasant note and he was unquestioning in the set-up of the next meeting. I arrived at the café to find him already seated. I was carrying a shopping bag full of photocopied articles, a few research journals and some larger published annotated research bibliographies. I could see that he was happy to see me, until he saw the bag of written material.

We chatted for a short while about the local news and made small talk about the weather. Finally, I put the large, full bag on the table. "Here is the research for you. These are all about the effectiveness of energy healing, prayer, and spiritual forms of treatment. I am sure you'll find something of interest."

Somewhat defeated in his tone, Dr. Carl looked at me. "The truth is that I don't want to read this stuff. Frankly, I just don't *want* to believe in these things. I am really not prepared to change the way I think. I realize how that may sound, but I am just not willing to consider the possibility that seriously."

"Oh!" I felt relieved. "Well, as long as you can admit it's a matter of belief and not evidence, I can respect that. I have no need to convert you, and I'll be better off if you have no need to convert me."

Our lunch ended soon after and I was surprised to detect a note of what felt like sadness in his final response to the topic. It was as if he felt he failed himself as a scientist when he realized how bound he was by belief. In many ways, he was responding much like the people he criticizes. For me, it was a tremendous lesson in the importance of willingness and openness in the experience of Ordinary Magic.

We experience Ordinary Magic when we personally witness or are impacted by an action or an event that defies our assumptions about the basic laws of nature. In these moments, it is as if these things have happened "by magic" or as a miracle. Even science struggles to explain these phenomena. Ordinary Magic is the realm of the unexplainable and the mysterious. Exposure to such stories, and whether we listen with prejudice or consideration is a choice. One that many are not ready to make.

Some people would argue it is safer and wiser to be sceptical and cynical, rather than gullible, seeking magic, or easily impressed. Ultimately, you have more choice over your attitude and what you focus on than what you may feel. Open-mindedness, willingness, and intent are actual skills by which we may notice and appreciate Ordinary Magic more and more.

As we go and grow along the spiritual path we sometimes change our feelings about such encounters. Some things that once sounded ridiculous or impossible begin to sound appealing or worthy of consideration. Some things once magical, one day become commonplace. Sometimes we witness the power of a person's mind over their body, or we experience their ability to move energy in others or the world and it truly seems extraordinary. Years later we ourselves become the master of time, space, and energy, and new things seem like magic. The heart of an experience of Ordinary Magic is the witnessing of things that defy logic and your worldview. There is a sense of awe and mystery at events occurring in the natural world. In that moment we may feel we have glimpsed the proof that there is something more to this world than what we see. We realize that there may indeed be a Sacred Dimension to all things.

When and Where?

Experiences of Ordinary Magic typically occur when you notice any of the following happening:

- You experience a spontaneous physical healing that is unexpected and unexplained.
- A dream or premonition comes true.
- You witness or personally experience unexplainable intuition (clairvoyance, clairsentience, etc.).
- You experience a meaningful and profoundly unlikely synchronicity (coincidence).
- Someone says what you are thinking.

- You think of something before it happens.
- You experience an undeniable outcome from a spiritual technique you previously did not believe in fully, such as prayer, or a form of "energy healing."
- Unexplainable events in extreme settings, such as being saved during an accident or war, such as people surviving impossible odds.
- You experience something that feels like a miracle or a complete mystery that evokes a sense of awe.

The Power to Heal

I once met a woman, Sara, who told me a story about going for a hike with her young nine-year-old daughter. At one point, her daughter became excited by a beautiful butterfly and ran off the trail to chase it. Before Sara could react, her daughter Christy stumbled and fell down a slope at the edge of the trail. Christy collided forcefully against a large sharp rock and cut her leg badly.

Sara raced to her daughter's side in absolute terror. She had no medical training and could now see the terrible gash, more than four inches long, and bleeding profusely. Sara became choked up as she told the story. "I didn't know if she broke her leg, or was going to bleed to death before I could carry her back to the car. The wound looked so awful. There was so much blood."

Sara went on to explain that the first thing she thought to do was to calm her daughter and herself. She tells of how she dusted her off, sat her on her lap and used her baseball cap to cover the wound. As Christy stopped crying, she began to relax. Slowly her awareness began to expand as the sounds of birds and the warmth of the sun caught her attention.

The wound was still bleeding uncontrollably from under the hat. Hours away from help, Sara felt a welling-up of guilt and regret for what she felt was her poor judgment. She thought she should not have taken her daughter on such a long walk, she should have had a first aid kit, a cell phone. As she began to lose herself in thoughts of what to do next, her daughter spoke up. "Mommy, just put your hands on it. You can fix it." Sara was shocked.

At first she thought her daughter was just thinking like a child. Then she was overcome by the thought that maybe she *could* help her. Sara, who had no training in or exposure to any form of healing work took the hat off the still bleeding, and now swelling wound and she placed her right hand upon it. She closed her eyes, took deep breaths and with all her heart and soul prayed to send what she called "healing energy and light" into her daughter's wound. She pictured it healing quickly, she pictured it as it was before the fall. Christy also closed her eyes.

When Sara opened her eyes her daughter was asleep against her shoulder and the wound had completely stopped bleeding. There was still a terrible tear in the skin, but the wound seemed a bit smaller, the redness was gone and the blood was quickly drying around it. She woke her daughter and asked if she could get up. As she got to her feet, her daughter said that the pain was gone and that she was ready to go home. They cleaned the cut a little more with the last of their bottled water and headed back to the car.

Sara was amazed to see that not only did the cut cease to bleed or ache on the way back to the car, but that when she took her daughter to the doctor late that afternoon, he remarked that it appeared to be several days old. He asked why she didn't bring her in sooner, saying that if he had seen it at the time of the accident he might have recommended stitches. Sara explained that it had only happened around noon earlier in the day. She says her doctor had nothing to say to her in response. He was silent for a long time. He remarked to little Christy, "You are a very lucky little girl; this could have been a terrible scar. But something seemed to have helped. It's curious." He turned to Sara once more, "You are sure you didn't put anything on this?" Christy added, "Of course! She used her love to heal it. I told her to."

Sara tells me that years later there is still no sign of scarring and both remember that day vividly.

Miracles or Super-Science?

Stories and experiences of Ordinary Magic have a built-in complexity. Like Sara's story, in many cases they require an element of willingness to be surprised, suspension of disbelief, and feeling or faith that the world may indeed operate according to more mysterious principles than we yet understand. Many people doubt these stories and feel sure that they must be embellished. Nevertheless, the medical literature is full of unexplainable stories of healing. It is not full, however, of magical explanations. That would be foolish in the eyes of science. Or would it be?

When I worked in hospital settings and shared stories like this, I was often flooded by accounts from nurses and doctors who also seemed to have multiple stories of extreme and unexplainable healings; stories of people who knew when they'd die; people who knew if they'd live; people who swore to have visits from mysterious healers who removed their illness; people whose intention and will alone beat unimaginable odds. I have met several people whose cancers have unexplainably abated and even dissolved against all odds. I have witnessed people who have been healed through ceremonies and the power of community, compassion, and prayer. I myself am one such person.

In his amazing 1992 publication, *Future of the Body*, Michael Murphy documents a great range of documented and yet unexplained phenomena of the human body and mind. Yet what he offers is an inventory, not an explanation, although the collection points to one simple glaring possibility: that the mechanics of healing and knowing, are not limited to the physical world we easily measure. Norman Shealy M.D., Ph.D., Larry Dossey M.D. and Daniel Benor M.D., are three authors that have compiled both stories and evidence of miraculous healing, and there are many others. Science cannot explain all the mysteries of the world that exist, still, we know that such amazing things do exist. It is why we have the words "miracle" and "magical." More than anything, they refer to events that have no *rational* material explanation.

The field of mind–body medicine has grown tremendously in recent decades and is sinking deep roots in esteemed medical programs such as those at Harvard, University of San Francisco, Stanford, and Duke. Ancient and modern healing techniques based on the concept of subtle energy and the power of awareness and intention are commonly used around the world today. Lissa Rankin M.D., Daniel J. Benor M.D., James Oschman Ph.D., Larry Dossey M.D., Richard Gerber M.D., and Norman Shealy M.D. are all examples of clinically trained professionals who have worked to survey and popularize the incredible power and possibility of these healing techniques.

Most people have encountered things that they tried but could not explain. Some people rationalize these moments by pointing to coincidence, wishful thinking, and poor judgment. It is also true, that sometimes no explanation is an invitation to take science further. As we allow for the convergence of science and spirituality, we find the benefits lie not in justifying spiritual truths, but putting them to work in the world for the betterment of our lives and the world.

The power of intention and prayer is one such case. It is easy for people who are spiritual and religious to envision the power and importance of prayer. The astounding advances in documenting the mind's ability to impact events at a distance shows us that prayer, intention, and meditation have a healing power greater than placebo alone. Authors like Gregg Braden, Michael Talbot Ph.D., and Deepak Chopra M.D. have done a great deal to document and publish information about such phenomena. A host of studies show that "mere" thoughts and feelings have the ability to influence systems, like bacteria or white blood cells, at a distance. There is also preliminary evidence to suggest that the same ability can influence large systems, such as human populations. One famous study showed that crime rates in a city were reduced when a critical mass of people were meditating at the same time.

Too often we hear such studies and stories and say we "want to believe," but continue living as if we don't. The irony is that the willingness to be actively looking for Ordinary Magic builds a mindset that helps it to become more evident in your life. For most, until a moment of Ordinary Magic happens to us, and until it changes our life in a radical way, we often find ways to overlook the possibilities. Though academics and authors search for the science behind Ordinary Magic, it is the mystery that intrigues them, and ultimately it is the mystery that outweighs their ability to explain all that we encounter.

Self-Science: The Practical Side of Things

Another common area of mystery and practical application is intuition, which is not about impacting things at a distance—but knowing things at a distance. When I teach about intuition, skeptics suggest that intuitive thoughts are just quick subconscious formulations of information we have already encountered. I have experienced too many gifted intuitives, including my spiritual father *Wanagi Wachi*, and my Venda African teacher *Chivengwa* to doubt this. As a healer *Chivengwa* has an uncanny ability to dream of his clients before they even arrive for help. I have seen this with my own eyes and watched as he prepared the medicine for a man nearly eight hours before he arrived.

I must admit, however, it took me a long time to overcome my doubt. One experience after another, my resistance and skepticism was washed away. To face my doubts and consider a new truth I needed to be open to a self-science. This means to look at my own experiences and beliefs about them objectively and with openness to consider new things. I started to write down dreams more often and payed attention to synchronicities. Eventually, I began to develop a sense of difference between dreams that were about my own psychological process and dreams that were about the world around me and things about to happen.

I recall a very important career transition I made when I was a young department director in an inner city hospital in Canada. I made an appointment to meet with the CEO of our entire healthcare regional organization—30,000 staff and over 120 sites of care. I had a vision for a new program to support staff and introduce more principles of holistic and compassionate care to the system. The night before, I dreamt of our meeting and conversation. Key words jumped out: legacy, victims, and healing healthcare. The next day when we met I was sure to use all the phrases and key words from my dream. I explained how it felt to me like healthcare needed healing and that staff everywhere feel unsupported, overworked, and like victims in their own system. I questioned what legacy our generation of leaders (him) would leave behind.

His reply was breathtaking.

"I have been thinking the exact same things," he said. "I still practice as a physician part-time and I see exactly what you are talking about and I think about it all the time. Why do they feel like victims? That's the word I use. Can we create a healing healthcare movement and leave the community and this organization empowered for the next generation. That's a legacy as significant as providing good care just for today."

Within a month this CEO had set up a new budget for healing healthcare programs and within two months I took the office beside him as the first Senior Director of Organizational Development. It felt like a miracle.

To this day I watch for dreams that resonate with that sense of something more. Both my wife Uxia and I had dreams about our daughter before she was born, and even though doctors had told us it was unlikely we'd conceive, and even though we had been to fertility clinics to test the doubts and found the concerns confirmed, we knew that she was coming one day. More than than that, dreams told us about her personality and name long before we met her, and it all matched up extraordinarily.

Ultimately, the experience of Ordinary Magic is not about proof. It is not about proof of the miraculous, nor is it about the cutting-edge sciences that help us to understand it all. The experience is about defying the mind and the ego, and opening the heart. The gift of a moment of Ordinary Magic is that it connects us to a *felt sense* of the grandeur and awesome capacity of life and Spirit.

Exercise

For one week, place your attention on the extraordinary. Ask your friends and relatives, if they can think of examples of stories of things they experienced but could not explain. Ask for a story of something unexplainable that they experienced—a dream, a shocking coincidence, a miracle healing or chance meeting. You can prompt them with examples of synchronicities, dreams or intuitions that came true; unexplainable things they have seen in nature; people they know that experienced healing; or other similar phenomena. Be respectful and supportive when you ask. Many people are embarrassed by such moments, or have tried to forget them. See how many stories of Ordinary Magic you can come up with. Pay attention to synchronicities during this process.

The Real Gift

Ordinary Magic tames the ego and the mind while opening the heart to consider that our universe exists within a great mystery that is alive and working through us and with us. The true gift of these experiences is not the power to predict the future or the ability to avoid illness forever, but the peace that comes with knowing that we can release our drive to control life and its events and trust that a turn for the better is always possible; sometimes even in the darkest moments. Once we know that we are not in control, nor can we ever have all the answers, it gives us permission to relax, to observe, and be a co-creator along with life and The Sacred.

Many renowned spiritual leaders around the world, often warned against the pursuit of supernatural powers, lest we forget their source and origin. Many masters I have met along the way have echoed the same sentiment. While in China for a very short time I managed to visit a few temples and sacred sites. In one temple off the coast of Hong Kong I met a monk who stopped to greet me and asked if I had any questions of the place I was visiting. His English was quite clear and he was clearly accustomed to managing the tourist visitors.

I wondered how he felt he was treated by tourists and if he felt there were misconceptions about his life and practice. We got to talking about Western stereotypes of Eastern masters and martial arts. For some reason, I mentioned the movie "Crouching Tiger, Hidden Dragon," which, of course he had not seen (I don't think he had seen much of any film in his life). We started to talk about the power of mind control, and whether human beings really have the ability to do miraculous things, such as endure extreme temperatures, foretell the future, move objects with the mind, walk on water, and so on. To him these incredible acts were only a matter of skill and knowledge. He had no doubts. As I got excited by the conversation, he seemed to retreat. At one point he became quiet. I began to feel uncomfortable. Finally, he responded.

"My friend, I have seen and I have been told of many such 'miracles.' They are not miracles, they are the forgotten powers natural to a mind that is awake and disciplined. Most people only dream of what is possible; the ancient masters *did it.*

"Healing, flying, seeing the future, it is all possible. But, I will tell you what my teacher told me. No special power or talent is as mighty as the loving heart and the quiet mind. Many people who master these secret arts that you are so interested in become lost. Their power becomes their God. Their talent feeds their ego. If you ever are blessed to see or maybe one day do such things, remember this. Magic will not bring you joy. Magic's power is that it points you beyond the physical world. Let it be a reminder *not* of how powerful we are as human beings, but of how vast this universe is. Then, let it all go. Any attachment creates suffering—even attachment to miracles."

That brief meeting touched me deeply, and I will never forget those words. I knew in my heart I was seeking magic and miracles in the world. Maybe it was to feel more powerful, maybe to enjoy the thrill of surprise and the unknown. That message has stayed with me to this day, for it is the teaching of Ordinary Magic. When magic and miracles show themselves, embrace them. If the evidence is clear, and the explanation is not, do not doubt them. More than healing or influence over others, the real gift is cultivating a sense of wonder, curiosity, open-mindedness, and the knowledge that this world is more mysterious than you will ever know, and you are a part of that miracle.

Chapter Four

The Experience of the Spirit World

*When we learn to open our lives to the Spirit World we
encounter the complexity of consciousness
and a source of wisdom, relationship, and power that is ever-present.
In those experiences we feel guided and connected to larger family.
We learn that love is never lost, and we cease to feel alone.*

Swallowed by the Spirit

During my first trip to Mexico, I stayed with a friend of mine, *Quetzal*, a Mayan shaman. A shaman is a healer whose primary mode of healing involves the direct communication with the world of Spirits and Natural Spiritual Powers. For *Quetzal*, like all the Indigenous shamans I know, his gift to heal and connect with the Spirit World was neither chosen nor taught. It was an ability directly given through dreams, extraordinary events and natural talents. *Quetzal's* mission is to bridge the modern world with the wisdom of the past for the healing of the future. His style of teaching and helping reflects the ancient roots of his ancestors.

Shortly after I arrived, *Quetzal* said there was a place that I needed to go in order to truly connect with and understand his ancestors: *Teotihuacán*. Only then, once my spirit was acknowledged by the spirits of his ancestors could we continue in our time together attending ceremonies and meeting other shamans. Following his direction, I made a special trip to *Teotihuacán* with his sister, Gia, a gifted spiritual healer and intuitive.

Teotihuacán is an astonishing and enormous ancient place of ceremonial pyramids, temples, and community living areas. Not far from Mexico City, the entire settlement is organized and laid out according to sacred geometry, astrological patterns and intricate spiritual formulas and teachings. It has been the site of great spiritual ceremonies and pilgrimages for centuries, and it has been the subject of intense historical and anthropological study.

"I will show you how we approach this holy place, as a Mayan. Not as a tourist," Gia asserted. "If you know how to see, how to feel, you will know the secrets of this place." We stopped before entering the site, made prayers, placed a simple offering of tobacco on the earth and set our intentions clearly in our hearts. Our intention was to be open to whatever healing channels of awareness might help us to encounter the depth of this amazing and powerful place, and to enter with respect for the ancestors of the place.

Near the beginning of our journey into the sacred structures, we entered a special temple. Not one of the mighty pyramids, but another place. It was canyon-like and I immediately felt a sense of "energy" or a presence as we entered. It was as if there was a subtle hum, or vibration I could feel in my body. We found a place to sit that felt comfortable, safe, and centered. I noticed the ancient carvings, the sculptures and felt their deep significance though I did not understand them.

Once settled, Gia reached into her bag and pulled out a few ritual objects and set them between us. She instructed me to close my eyes, breathe deeply and to place my awareness in my heart, and then to simply allow my mind to be open to whatever might come to me. While I focused on the task I was given, she sang a prayer song I did not know or understand and then we both fell silent.

After an indistinguishable time, something changed. Suddenly, I began to see images with my eyes closed. The images became so vibrant; I could see and feel them as if they were real. A great snake, as thick as a bus and longer then I could see, appeared clearly in my mind—like a daydream, unfolding in front of me and yet not quite fully physical. It had a ring of rainbow-colored feathers around its neck. Its scales appeared to be a dark blue-green, almost black, but as it moved, the light revealed a dull but distinct rainbow hue, like one would see in a soap bubble.

I watched as it moved with ease and power through a dense jungle. It dove into the land, as if the earth were water. It traveled huge distances in moments. I followed its journey as it roamed the ancient lands of central America. It moved from temple to temple and then dove into the earth again. This time, when it surfaced, it shot straight up into the sky and flew. It circled right above us.

Though my eyes remained closed, it felt as if I was watching something that was actually taking place at that very moment. Suddenly, the great snake plummeted to the earth, jaws open, and it consumed me, in one sweeping movement. My mind went dark as I felt more than I saw. Now I was in the heart of this mighty being. Somehow, I became the heart of the land. I felt the people, the spirits, the sacred places all inside me. It was as if Mexico, its people, its history and its guiding spirits were swimming within me. Suddenly, my awareness shifted again and I was observing the earth as if in outer space, and the earth became a brilliant ball of white shining light. Then everything became still.

At this time, Gia had begun to pray out loud. I opened my eyes and my attention turned to her. Tears were rolling down her cheeks. I could not understand her fast-paced Spanish, and her strong emotions made it even harder to follow. Then, her disposition shifted and her words became less passionate; softer. Strong, like the delivery of a message, but gentle as if the message was precious. I sat and absorbed the moment—surprised, but profoundly moved.

When Gia came to her normal awareness I was ready and waiting to hear what had happened, and eager to tell her about what happened to me. She asked me to tell her what I saw first, since it seemed to have catalyzed what had happened to her. I told her of the enormous snake, and all that I saw. She was so intent, so serious, and then smiled. "That is *Quetzalquatl*, one of our most powerful gods. This place we are in is his temple, where the ancient people came to communicate with him. You have seen him, you have been received by him." At this point I went from surprised to speechless.

Encounters of the Spirit World

Prior to that moment in Mexico, I had not consciously had any awareness of the divine being called Quetzalquatl. I may have overheard something along the way, but nothing I could think of could explain what I experienced or its significance to the people I was traveling with. Working with my Lakota dad *Wanagi Wachi* over the years, I had certainly been around many events that involved Spirits and Spiritual Beings, but I tended to assume that they were either projections of the mind, or fascinating realities that I'd personally never encounter. The more I reflected on that experience in the temple, the more I came to question this possibility. Is there a Spirit World, full of beings, ancestors, angels, and deities that actually have a substance and existence independent of human thought?

I felt like I was standing at a crossroads. It seemed like the age-old question: if a tree falls in the forest and no one is there to hear it, does it still make a sound? Was I so egocentric to believe that just because I didn't see or experience Spiritual Beings that they did not exist? I have not been to Milwaukee or Moscow, and yet I believe they exist. People tell me of their experiences, and I trust that the lives of people in Moscow and Milwaukee were unfolding without a hitch even when I did not know they existed. Could the Spirit World be so real, so close? Just a journey away?

For the remainder of that trip to Mexico, I took every reference to a Spirit seriously and literally. My experience of ceremonies, dreams, and prayers was transformed forever. Even a trip to the Museum of Anthropology took on new meaning for me. The ancient images, carvings, and art are more than superstitious, more than symbolic, they are a language that expresses a living relationship with the Spirit World. The idea of a Spirit Being was taking form in my mind and my life in a way it never had before.

On the plane ride home I thought about the people I had known who had encountered Spirit Beings. Naturally, all the Native healers I knew fell into this category, but then there were family and friends as well. I recalled the time my sister and her partner woke up in the middle of the night to *see* a woman holding a baby at the foot of their bed. Neither she nor he had seen anything like this before. Much like in the movies, this translucent vision was shared by both of them, at the same time. They recounted how they both looked on in surprise and disbelief—despite what was before their eyes.

I thought of a friend of mine, Darren, who had told me that since a young age he had always been able to see spirits as lights. Darren never struck me as crazy. He held down a normal job and was in perfect health. All the cultures I had encountered, all seemed to have talked about spirits. All were in relationship to the Spirit World. It had never impacted me like this experience of my own. The list of encounters and believers grew and grew in my mind until I began to feel absurd for *not* seriously considering it all. From that moment I gave myself permission to acknowledge, from my heart, the existence of a world of Spiritual Beings. Most importantly, I offered my permission for that world to touch my life. Without a doubt, it has.

Today, the Spirit World is a large part of my life, though it is still not something I experience as immediately as others do. I am not a shaman or a professional medium. I am dear friends with many mediums, channels, psychics, and clairvoyants, and I respect those who have a refined gift for such work. In fact, as a Hay House author, I find many of my colleagues have been able to build their careers upon the ability to communicate with the Spirit World. I have seen first-hand how many of these people have brought impossible and life-changing messages to people from the "other side."

I have even become acquainted with a number of Spirit Beings directly myself. I have learned much about Spiritual Beings and how to release their impositions and gain their loving support. I even run ceremonies that help people to honor and connect with their ancestors and Spiritual Guides. Regardless of the setting or the approach, one message from the Spirit World comes consistently to me, again and again: "Don't forget us. We are here and waiting to help. Just ask. People forget their ancestors. They have forgotten us. They have forgotten that we love you and that we can help."

What Is the Spirit World?

In an experience of the Spirit World, people have direct contact with a range of beings that are non-physical, intelligent, and sentient (conscious). This dimension is very complex and its facets are beyond counting. It includes all spiritual beings from ghosts to angels, and even Gods, and personal forms of God. Anything that has a personal nature and has characteristics such as will, intelligence, personality, form, face, conscious intent, and/or a distinct presence falls into the category of Spirit World.

The very quality of "identity" is very specific to this realm of experience. People who have personal encounters of God, such as the feeling that Jesus is walking beside them, or a vision of the Divine Mother Mary or Krishna–they are having an experience of this quality. For some, the encounter is so radical, real and deeply personal it is nearly impossible to consider that there are other such encounters happening all the time, all over the world. It is easy to trust what we know and fear what we do not.

In nearly every spiritual tradition there is a pantheon of spiritual beings. Christian, Jewish and Islamic angels, ascended Saints and Prophets; Indigenous animal and nature spirits; Hindu Gods and Goddesses; Tibetan Buddhist deities, and all other sacred beings of all traditions are within this category of experience. Any *personal* God concept or experience can also be placed in this category.

This is why the mystics within most traditions claim that any God that can be conceived of as form, is not the totality of God. For example, when I write the word "God," I am not referring to any one God, but the totality of all that is—including all created life, all invisible existence, all Spirits and images of God. All are Sacred; all are expressions of God as the Oneness of all things. Relations to an infinite and eternal "Oneness" is a bit challenging for the heart and mind to grasp, so we use metaphors, images, characteristics, and our encounters of the Divine Beings, to describe what we are relating to. Yet any Spirit Being, any God, is just an aspect of a Greater Sacred Mystery.

It can be difficult for people to learn that their personal picture of God can be placed into a category inhabited by millions of others. This reveals one of the limits of personal divinities and our deeply personal relationships to them: we think they must be the only one. If we look to the original teachings within the world's traditions we see that Krishna is God, and yet only an aspect of God. We see that Jesus is God and yet only the Son of God. We find the Buddha venerated, and yet teaches that true awakening requires his students to transcend him. The enlightened masters all knew, that even the face of the Divine, is just a mask. They knew that the Infinite Sacred Source is revealed in the expressions of Spiritual beings and yet is above them all.

Afraid of Ghosts?

Some people find it difficult and threatening to even consider experiencing *any* invisible being, including the idea that God could be revealed in a form like Jesus, Vishnu, or Quezatcoatl.

If they have come to believe in a picture of the world that does *not* include beings without physical bodies, the unexpected arrival of a spiritual visitor in a dream, waking vision, or moment of spiritual practice can be unnerving and even concerning.

Over the years I have worked with many clients who had no choice but to believe in the existence of Spirits due to voices, visions, or a presence in their home they could not explain or avoid. Some Spirit visits can be so "real" and emotionally potent that people become confused or scared. Many people fear these experiences with such intensity that they will either rationalize the encounter away, or they will avoid all things related to the trigger of the experience.

It can be the end of spiritual practice for some people altogether. I know of one woman whose experiences of the Spirit World were so strong and confusing as a teenager that she consciously shut down any attention to her intuition and dreams until she was in her forties. Anything that could leave her open to experiences of the Spirit World, she avoided. Without a supportive council or a culture that understood her, she felt isolated and in fear of her mental health. Sometimes we just can't deny our experience, and yet we cannot embrace or admit it either.

I have had many clients who have been awakened in the middle of the night to find a spirit of one kind or another in their room. More amazing is how often two or more people awake to encounter the same exact thing. A client once told me that the day after her mother's funeral she and her husband woke up startled to find a white bird flying around their bedroom. The husband got out of bed to find the open window that allowed the bird in, and chase it out. He found no open window, but came back to the bedroom to find his wife in tears. The bird had vanished right before her eyes. She knew it was her mother, coming to say goodbye. The husband, on the other hand, was frustrated and angered by the event. "It is not possible," he said as he returned to bed, "It just can't be." They never found an open door or window, and a bird has never before or since entered their home. Her husband prefers not to talk about it all.

It is difficult to know what to do with experiences of the Spirit World. For some people asking for help is too embarrassing. In a culture that favors science as the dominant religion, such encounters are always doubted or rationalized away. People who experience the Spirit World are frequently made to feel wrong or deluded. The resistance to the Spirit World is predominant in the Western world. While other cultures around the world may not encourage the experience of the Spirit World, the vast majority accept its existence.

Not long after my trip to Mexico when I encountered the god Quetzalquatl I was in South Dakota preparing for a *Hanblecha*, Vision Quest, ceremony. Having fasted in isolation in the wilderness a number of times before in the same ceremony, I was not feeling anxious or concerned about the days ahead. It was the night before and we had just finished our last *Inipi*, Sweat Lodge purification ceremony, in preparation. Everyone had left the ceremonial site in the country and headed back to the small town nearby where most of them lived. I stayed behind to clean up the area and be sure I had myself ready for the next day's departure to my fasting site.

The night sky was moonless and magnificent. Not a cloud in the sky, the stars arched across the heavens in a great embrace. The evening was peaceful, the fire was nearly out and I knelt beside it to offer a final prayer in preparation. I asked that I would finally be able to see and encounter the Spirit World directly myself. So many of the mentors, healers, and spiritual teachers I had known were familiar with the world of Spiritual Beings. Many could see, hear, or feel such beings with ease. I wanted to experience it myself. I had longed for this. I had prayed for this, ever since I had learned to accept the possibility.

I finished up, climbed into my truck and began the trip back down the gravel country roads to town. I was listening to music on the radio and savoring the gentle weight of the night, when I thought I saw something fly across the road right in front of me. I was alert and looking. It seemed there was a strange hum coming from within the truck or outside. I shut off the music and slowed down. The hum remained. It was not the truck; it seemed like it was outside, and it seemed like it was in my head. I pulled off to the side of the road and stopped.

It was more like a feeling now. A sound I could hear, but not with my ears, like the ringing vibration you might feel after standing next to a loud speaker or heavy machinery. The feeling was intense and I could not understand what was happening. I stepped out of the truck and on to the road. The night sky still brilliant, I looked up into the endless depth. Then I felt it.

It was like I was being watched. Looking toward the sky I saw a set of eyes. Maybe I felt a set of eyes. It is hard to say. And then, another. And another. It was like a great veil was slowly being drawn away and a countless chorus of creatures were staring down at me, more and more. The air was thick with energy. The profound sense of how real the beings were was overwhelming, for it was still apparent that there was nothing physically different above or around me. The incomprehensibility and immensity of the feeling became more than I could bare. I felt naked, watched, surrounded by countless forms I did not understand. I hurried back into the truck and prayed, "Please, please, it is too much! I don't need to see anything, only what you want me to see, I am happy with my life as it is. I don't need to see all this, please!!"

The hum in my ears stopped. The density of the night lifted, and as if I woke up from a dream, I became aware of the gentle cricket songs, the fresh summer breeze, and the grace of the stars above. All was well. I continued my drive in to town and wondered what I had asked for; what I had received? I felt my arrogance in wanting to command something I did not understand. I felt a power I did not understand, and remembered the wisdom of the veil between worlds. I understood the reason for ceremony, ritual, and teachings of those who know the Spirit World. There is an order, a design, even in the world beyond worlds.

Experience Changes Everything

I was not raised to believe in Spirits or ghosts. As a Jewish person, I hadn't even thought of a God that had a face or body. I thought all such concepts were only metaphors and psychological creations—until I started to experience them myself. The most striking of such experiences that I have had did not even match my culture or even my own capacity to create a self-deception. The experiences were often shocking or unexpected. They challenged my assumptions about the world to such an extreme that I have at times been terrified during my encounters. Fear, doubt, and resistance are common reactions amongst people who do not "believe" in spirits, ghosts, and angels. I certainly had my share of those reactions. Naturally, it depends on the setting and the experience.

I have learned that in the Spirit World we can encounter many things that we do not know, for these things have their own "being," their own nature, their own energy. They are real, independent of our minds and imaginations. In part, this is why so many people get stuck on "their" vision and version of God, gods and goddesses. They have experienced a distinct and personal connection to something that seems whole and complete. It feels as real as anything else, and it seems unlikely there could be anything else so fantastic or amazing. It is hard enough to imagine that there are other divinities and deities than the ones we have been introduced to. It is even harder to realize that these beings are not the totality of the Spirit World, or God. Even a personal image of God is a limited image of God. The depth of God, The Sacred, is revealed in spiritual experiences and qualities we are not yet aware of.

What's It Like?

When people encounter a Spiritual Being, they typically have all the self-awareness, power of choice, and integrity that they choose to have. People often encounter Spirit Beings while fully awake. Sometimes the awareness of such a being comes in a dream or in a half-asleep moment, but it can occur in broad daylight. Usually there is an experience of some form of communication; it could happen in words, ideas that feel transmitted, or a felt-sense. There is also typically an unusually strong emotion and sensation that goes with the experience.

There are a few extreme reactions that are surprisingly common. The first is an overwhelming sense of a felt-presence (like a person standing behind you) and an accompanying sense of peace. People often say they felt "them" near and knew that "everything will be okay in their life." Another common and dramatic reaction is paralysis. A surprise visit from a Spirit Being often leaves people literally feeling as if they cannot move. Sometimes it would seem this is out of fear; however, other times it seems that this has more to do with the energy and presence of the Spirit Being itself. In either case, it is important to know that this is normal and should it happen to you, try to relax, breathe deeply, and remember you are still in control of yourself and your own mind.

The presence of a divine being, such as an encounter with the personal dimension of God, can be overwhelming with emotion and energy. It can be much like a strong physical vibration that is so intense it becomes hard to maintain a sense of personal identity or balance. I learned most of what I know about Spirit Beings from Indigenous and Hindu teachers; however, I am also aware that many of the biblical descriptions of prophets and angels are congruent with the perspective I have outlined here.

Ultimately, it's a personal sense. Everyone experiences these phenomena in slightly or dramatically different ways. In the presence of a spirit, for example, I tend to feel either a fever-like heat in my body, starting in my stomach and lower spine and moving upward, or all the hair on my arms will stand up on end, and I suddenly feel like crying.

I have friends who see them as flashes of light, and some are able to hear them as well. My mentors like *Wanagi Wachi* and *Chivengwa* also encounter them often. At times *Wanagi Wachi* is able to see, hear and interact with them. Some great mediums and spiritual guides never "see" Spirit Beings, but can easily hear and communicate with them. There is no rule or predictability—that is the only rule. It seems impossible to predict or measure the involvement of Spirits in our lives.

What Might We Encounter in the Spirit World?

Though not a complete inventory, encounters of the Spirit World may include direct contact with:

- Ghosts
- Ancestors
- Angels
- Ascended Masters
- Supreme God in a human form (such as Christ, the Virgin Mary, or Krishna)
- Gods and Goddesses
- Sacred Beings of Light and Energy
- Mythological Beings (such as a Thunder Being, or a Deer Woman)
- Animal Spirits
- Councils and Communities of Sacred Beings
- Fairies and "Little People"

Now What?

Just because you see a ghost, angel, or a Spiritual Being doesn't mean you have to do everything they say, or change your faith or religion. As an example, the above described experience endeared me deeply to the spirit of Quetzalquatl and the Mayan people, yet, it did not change my heritage, or style of worship, for I knew it was only one experience of one of millions of possible beings.

Despite what skeptics say, research with mediums (people who serve as communicators for the Spirit World) shows that there is significant evidence that people can communicate with the deceased. Furthermore, successful mediums point out that many Spirit Beings have agendas, preferences and personalities, and as such should not be thought of as all-knowing or perfect just because they no longer have a body.

To learn more about relating to the Spirit World it is helpful to learn from people who have a natural aptitude for experiencing the Spirit World. Certain people are born with a talent for seeing and feeling the presence of such beings. Authors and teachers like Rolling Thunder, John Lame Deer, Blair Robertson, Hank Wessleman, Sonja Choquette, Sylvia Brown, Sandra Ingerman and John Holland have all documented their stories of living with the ability to see, feel or interact with spiritual beings. Millions of readers have embraced their work, not just out of a desire to believe, but also out of a desire to make sense of their own experiences.

Skeptics and Charlatans: The Problem of Proof

While I have no doubt that there are Spirit Beings, I have come upon no sufficient way of completely and effectively explaining what a Spirit Being is made of, where it lives, and how it can move between dimensions. There are mountains of metaphysical writings that do try to answer these questions and what matters is that you find a worldview that suits you.

In the Spirit World, we encounter divine symbols and archetypes of The Sacred. Spirit Forms are both psychological archetypes and real entities. Just as a "policeman" is an idea and a stereotype in your mind, there are real police officers. In the same way we may experience "God" and relate to it intimately, though it is not the totality of The Sacred—the Totality of God the Source.

The major complicating factor is not the metaphysical complexity of Spirit Beings, but the human complexity of relating to them. When you have experiences of Spirits, reflect on them, seek guidance. When you seek guidance, don't believe everything you are told. Be sure you find people you can trust to explore the experience.

There can be no doubt that the world is full of charlatans in all professions and fields of work. If a person can make a dollar doing something, there will be someone trying to take advantage of that opportunity. This means that everyone who does the same thing does not have the same motive, talent, or integrity. Whether you are relating to a priest, a medium, or a scientific skeptic, it is always important to consider their history, their claims, and their intention. Absolutism for and against the existence of the Spirit World has clouded the evidence and left many people making decisions based on belief alone.

Because communicating with Spirit Beings is subtle, subjective, and very much an art, it is easy for people who do communicate with Spirit Beings to allow their ego and preferences to interfere. It is important to believe, to have faith, and to trust in the possibility of Spirit interactions. It is also important to remain thoughtful, careful, and discriminating. Perhaps this complexity lies at the root of why communication with gods, goddesses, and higher beings has been relegated to special groups and secret societies over the years. There is a very reasonable concern for the misuse of Spirit relationships.

Conversely, science also shows a range of extreme reactions to the phenomena of Spirit Beings and encounters with Angels and Ancestors. Unfortunately, prominent skeptics seem to have a desire to prove paranormal experiences to be false. The very fact that they have a desire to prove such phenomena wrong and an active disbelief proves that they are incapable of objectively pursuing the subject. True science involves the suspension of belief or disbelief and the complete willingness to let evidence dictate results and conclusions.

As an example the once famous "Amazing Randi" made a lucrative career de-bunking psychics, magicians, healers, and mediums. On the one hand, I compliment his ability to expose frauds and financial pred- ators. On the other hand, having known people who have investigated the Amazing Randi's million dollar offer for anyone who can prove the verifiable existence of a supernatural talent, it is clear that his intent is to disprove applicants.

I read the fine print of the application to his contest and there are many limiting rules including the statement that they "will *not* accept claims of the existence of deities or demons/angels, the validity of exor- cism, religious claims, cloudbusting..." Naturally this helps to avoid reli- gious controversy, but it also restricts the spiritual element of paranormal experiences and talents.

Further the contract states, "This offer is not open to any and all per- sons. Before being considered as an applicant, the person applying must satisfy two conditions: First, he/she must have a 'media presence,' which means having been published, written about, or known to the media in regard to his/her claimed abilities or powers. This can be established by producing articles, videos, books, or other published material that specifically addresses the person's abilities. Second, he/she must produce at least one signed document from an academic who has witnessed the powers or abilities of the person, and will validate that these powers or abilities have been verified."

This statement alone disqualifies all the spiritual teachers I have known whose focus in life is community service and healing, not fame and fortune. I respect the right of the Amazing Randi to set limits and rules in his contest, yet people must not jump to the conclusion that just because no one has won the million dollars that it proves the non-exis- tence of the Spirit World and related phenomena.

The final area of debate lies in understanding the tools and techniques by which data is gathered about the Spirit World. Some scientists claim that if something is "real" it should be observable and measurable. However, the existence of something is not derived from its evidence and measurement. For most of history, human beings could only see a limited range of the color spectrum. Now we have ways of seeing infrared and ultraviolet with ease. These were colors and levels of light that we were previously unaware of. Nevertheless, we can safely assume that ultraviolet light was not created the day a man finally saw it with his own eyes.

Science may one day learn to see aspects of the Spirit World.

A Personal God

In most of the world, still today, the Spirit World is assumed to be a normal part of life. In a great many religions the Spirit World is the focus. Typically it shows up in attention to angels, saints, ancestors, and concepts of God that have human forms and attributes. The fixation on the Spirit World seems to emerge from the human tendency towards personal relationships and the desire for an emotional dimension to our Higher Power. It is also much easier to allow the ego and persona to be involved in a relationship in which we can project values and needs as we do in our relationships with other people.

Most Christian traditions and many devotional sects within other traditions, such as Bhakti Yoga in Hinduism, Pure Land Buddhism, Shintoism, Kabbalah in Judaism, Sufism in Islam, and many Indigenous communities, are focused on the Spirit World and what is learned from it. If you look within your own culture you will likely find a great community of people who believe in the Spirit World. While Judaism and Islam have both favored the formless dimensions of an ultimate Sacred Source, personal prayer remains common, and the assumption that God has human traits persists. The Christian tradition is based openly on the idea that God can exist in human form. Christ has become the central focus for most Christians, as has the Virgin Mary, yet neither define the totality of God—even in traditional theology.

Devotion to a Divine Being can be a potent spiritual practice, and can richly reflect our unique needs and styles. The caution is against basing our world view solely on the beings we have encountered alone, and denying the existence of others. This would be like denying the existence of cities you have never visited, or assuming that your family is the "best" in the world just because it is yours. This way of thinking may work for devotional practice in isolation, but not as an ultimate worldview or way of relating to others. When "our God" becomes the only one *exclusive* of others, hostility and division are quick to follow. Relationship to the Spirit World and devotional practices must strike a fine balance between deep immersion and heartfelt connection, and the deeper awareness of "higher" dimensions of The Sacred.

My Spirit World versus Yours

Sadly, due to a lack of direct experience and an ongoing actual spiritual practice, many people trust the Spirit Beings in their own culture, but not in those of others. I once worked with a medical doctor who was Catholic and a regular church attendee. I heard him once making a comment to a devout Catholic patient about his faith in Christ and the helping power of the saints. I also watched him scoff and express disbelief and concern when an Indigenous American patient told her nurses that she had been visited by her deceased aunty while in the hospital. I could not understand the difference.

In South Africa I had a funny experience while getting supplies in a small town near a village I was staying in, in the Northeast. A white South African store clerk was helping me find some items in her store. She asked what I was doing in South Africa. When she learned I was staying in a Venda African village, not knowing I was studying with Traditional healers, she remarked, "Watch out for those witchdoctors!

Those people can't be trusted. I think they are working with the devil. And their talk of spirits and ancestors! Oh! What nonsense. Keep yourself close to church (she didn't know I was Jewish) and ask that the Angels protect you. You can never be too careful around those people." Clearly, she felt her invisible, spiritual beings were better than theirs.

When I spoke with my Venda teacher about this event, he laughed. "These are only words: 'ancestors' and 'saints.' We who work to help people, we all pray to the same God, we are all helped by the same spirits. Some call them saints and some call them ancestors. But our ancestors help Christians, and their saints help me. It's humans that make distinctions. My ancestors are happy to help you, and I know that yours are happy to help me."

The Message of the Masters

Most people fall into the extremes of being either fearful and disbelieving, or fascinated by the Spirit World. If your goal is spiritual growth, then it is important to have a balanced view of this type of experience and not get caught up in extremes. Be open to the possibility of Spiritual Beings; be unafraid, respectful, and empowered should an encounter occur; and be committed to a consciousness that is free of preoccupations with any attachment—including ghosts and Gods.

What we learn as we deepen a healthy relationship to the Spirit World, is that Spirit Beings can bring us great meaning and even aid. The healing quality of these experiences is well known and a wonderful introduction can be found in the work of Brian Weiss M.D., Sandra Ingerman, and many others. Believing in a Spirit World and interacting with it through prayer, meditation, devotion, and ritual can lead to extraordinary and life-changing experiences.

The Spirit World can be an invaluable guide and support to us as we make our way along the spiritual journey. For those who give permission and intentionally interact with the Spirit World, there is great power and value. Guiding or "guardian" spirits, ancestors, and angels all may be called upon for guidance, advice, and protection. I have never heard of such a force or Being expecting to be "worshipped" or thought of as more important than God, The Sacred Source of all things.

After years of participating in the spiritual ceremonies of Indigenous people, I began to use the same patterns and practices as those I had learned. It became clear that the ceremonial world was really a technology for relating to the Spirit World and The Sacred. When my dad was diagnosed with cancer I began to take this technology more to heart. I wondered, "If the Indigenous American people can pray to their ancestors for help, can I pray to mine? Why do theirs help and mine don't or is it that I don't ask?"

I created a small ceremony, using a candle, a picture of my grandfather, a small cup of water, and a hand full of nuts both of which were set out as an offering. I took the time to pray to God, the Highest Power as I understood it, and asked for only good things to come of my prayers. I also asked for my ancestors to be available to me for help and assistance to my dad. I asked that only that which is of the light would be drawn in, and that I'd be protected from anything else. I wanted to be sure that I was safe and careful in my approach.

Then I called upon my grandfather directly, my dad's dad, who had been dead for about 14 years. I asked him to help my dad and to comfort him. Still newly diagnosed, I was sure that my dad was not the type of man to express much emotion or ask for help beyond what the doctor would order. My dad was as business-minded a person as I have known. He did not have any interest in spirituality and less in religion. The world was black and white for him and science the obvious measure of things.

The next day I received a call from my mom; she sounded upset.

"You won't believe what just happened this morning. Dad was sitting eating breakfast and he suddenly called me from the kitchen. From where he sat at the table, he was staring at the stove. He asked me if I saw his dad—grandpa! I looked but didn't see anything. I asked what he saw and he described in great detail what grandpa was wearing, how he looked, and where he stood.

"I asked him how he felt; at first he said he was a bit scared. Then after a short time of watching, he corrected himself, and said he felt fine. Peaceful. He said it made him feel good to see his dad. As suddenly as it had happened, it ended."

"Why do you sound upset" I asked, feeling elated at the synchronicity of this event the morning after my ceremony speaking to his dad. "Well," my mom replied, "I wanted to see him too! I believe in this stuff. He doesn't! That's not fair!" We laughed at the amazement of it all.

A relationship with a Spirit being can be deeply rewarding, and yet it can also be a distraction. If you have had or are having difficulty experiences with the Spirit World, do not worry, you are not necessarily losing your mind. You should, however, seek help from someone knowledgeable and credible. Your experiences of the Spirit World will generally lead you to a fuller experience of yourself and the Spiritual World.

The same principles apply to our personal relationships with God. When we place a face and personality upon the Divine, we gain access to that powerful dimension of divinity. At the same time, remember that anything that can be named, or described in words, cannot contain the totality of The Sacred. If the ultimate source of all things is eternal and infinite, then any and every idea used to discuss it is by its nature, limited.

When we learn to open our lives to the Spirit World we encounter the complexity of consciousness and a source of wisdom, relationship, and power that is ever-present. In those experiences we feel guided and connected to larger family. We learn that love is never lost, and we cease to feel alone.

Exercise

To begin, you must feel ready and willing to connect with a Spirit Being. Then simply choose one to three "spirit guides" you'd like to speak to. This list could include dead relatives, ancient masters like Jesus or Buddha, iconic beings like Mother Theresa or John Lennon, Crazy Horse or St. Francis. You can include angels, saints, or even Spirits of Nature.

Find some way to physically represent each being so that you can easily arrange and place them on a table beside where you will sit and write. Bring paper and a pen. Divide your page in three sections vertically, one for each guide. Then divide the page in three again. This way you have each name at the top and three sections below each.

Next, choose three questions you'd like to ask each. Write them down. You can write the questions into the top of each box if you are able or on another piece of paper. Keep the questions very clear, personal, and concise. Try simple questions like: what can I do to improve my relationship? why am I not happy at work? what do you want me to know about my health/my son/my job, etc. You can also ask big questions about the spirit world, but remember that the more specific questions will get clearer answers. Big broad cosmic questions may get answers that are harder to understand.

Find a quiet window of time to sit with your images of your guides and your paper. Start with a couple of minutes of slow, deep belly breaths. Breathe in and count 4, hold for a count of 4, breath out a count of 4, hold for a count of 4. Be purposeful, pay attention, feel yourself relax.

Once you are relaxed, pray. Pray in your own way, or simply talk to God and the Spirits you hope to contact and ask them to be with you, show respect and gratitude. Imagine they are present. Open your eyes, look kindly at the images of them and then simply begin to quickly and without much thought or complication, review each question and write the answer that immediately presents to you. Spirit answers tend to be very short and simple—one word or a sentence. If the answer is long or complex, it is likely your own mind in the way. Take a breath and start over.

This exercise is not perfect or easy for everyone, but it is a fun way to begin.

When you are finished, be sure to express gratitude whether you felt it worked or not and ask for signs and guidance in the days to come. Then, pay attention . . .

Chapter Five

The Experience of the Cosmic Self

In the experience of the Cosmic Self we become participants, not just observers, in the spiritual world. These experiences awaken us to the reality that consciousness, energy, and awareness form the foundational field of life.
We discover that we are first and foremost a soul of tremendous power, and that our bodies and five senses provide us with a wonderful but limited perception of the world.

The Freedom to Fly and More

Spring time in Winnipeg, Canada, was always an amazing experience for me. After months and months of a bitterly cold winter, the return of warm weather was always like a rebirth of the soul. Outside my bedroom window the world would change from waves of white, to a barren brown, and finally to a joyful and resilient green. Trees and grasses bloomed and triumphed everywhere.

One morning I stepped out into the backyard of the home I grew up in to take in the beauty of the early light. The rows of lilac bushes aroused my senses. The vibrant lawn and old spruce and birch trees seemed so welcoming. I was filled with the vitality of the day. I could feel it moving in me, as if I were a sprout of green life bursting from the earth. I felt like singing, like dancing. The energy was more than I could contain, and I leapt just to feel myself jump.

Effortlessly I left the ground, and found myself rising about 15 feet in the air and then landing gently back on the earth. I was shocked. I had never experienced something like this before. Again I sprang up, this time higher than the oldest tree; again floating easily to the ground. Then I jumped to the very top of the roof. I could see for miles. I could see rooftops; birds resting on power lines; traffic in the distance. This was my community. It was a beautiful day, but somehow I knew there was more. This new found ability was more than incredible, it was fun!

Without thinking, I leapt again, this time soaring into the sky; now free from gravity, free from the weight of earth. Effortlessly I moved through the clouds and open blue, crossing the countryside. It was more amazing than I could have imagined. Somehow I always knew this was possible. Watching below, I saw prairies, foothills, mountains, the great Pacific shoreline, and then the ocean. Playing with seagulls, I soared over the ocean until they caught my attention: whales! A huge mother and two younger whales, bigger than infants, but not quite full grown. They moved like planets through space: deliberate, with immense presence.

I dove into the deep silence of the water. Suddenly, everything slowed down. The bright blue world of sky vanished. Below me an immense darkness, above me giant shadows and moving bodies. The sun filtered down around the enormous and powerful creatures. I felt safe, protected and, somehow, guided. Their peace became my peace. The completeness I felt in them became my completeness. I dissolved into that moment and will never forget it.

When I awoke, it took some time to realize that this experience was a dream. I had many dreams of unusual things, and even dreams of things before they happened. But this was a dream where I was sure I was awake and I felt conscious of each choice I made! In it I was free from the laws of physics and I was very aware of it. Lucid dreams like this one are a part of the category of spiritual experience I call, "The Cosmic Self." In the experience of the Cosmic Self we experience ourselves as being masters of time, space, matter, and energy.

What Is the Cosmic Self?

Experiences of the Cosmic Self are unforgettable though less common than the first three experiences of The Sacred that we have discussed. In the first three types of experience (Truth and Beauty; Ordinary Magic; and The Spirit World) our perception of the world is challenged and changed. Our experience of our *self* and *identity* is essentially the same as always, clearer or deeper. When we are experiencing the first three types of Spiritual Awareness it can feel like we are being called to shed old ways that do not serve or represent us well. However, with the first three types of experiences we are often passive or inactive. We feel we are witnessing an extraordinary moment, though we do not feel responsible for it, or in control of it.

The Cosmic Self is an experience in which we become self-aware, active, and engaged in the spiritual dimensions of life. Creating synchronicity is a great example. When we encounter a surprising and unexpected set of impossible and meaningful coincidences, it becomes an experience of Ordinary Magic. It touches us deeply, and turns our attention toward The Sacred. In the Cosmic Self we set an intention and consciously influence timing and synchronicity in our lives. Some people call this "manifesting."

Dreams offer another good example. Over the years I have been visited by my spiritual teachers, or animal spirits, whereas my wife Uxia mostly has random psychological dreams and then infrequently and suddenly clear premonitions that come true. Mentors of mine, such as those in South Dakota and Venda, South Africa have the ability to ask for direct guidance before they sleep, and in their dreamworld very real concrete answers to very specific questions—usually about healing— will come to them. In fact, many of them can hold actual conversations with other "beings" while in the dream state.

The Experience of the Cosmic Self is a radical departure from any-thing "normal" and always qualifies distinctly as an altered state. Ordi-nary Magic is a more passive experience in the landscape of the material world. In the experience of the Cosmic Self we actually experience our-selves differently, and we inhabit an immaterial world. In the experience of the Cosmic Self our identity shifts, we no longer feel identified with our bodies or normal self-consciousness. Instead we identify with our soul as an independent energy and awareness that can move freely from the confines of everyday laws of thought and form. When we are "in" our Cosmic Self we may have new modes of sensing, the perception of new abilities that defy logic and physics, and a heightened experience of our normal five senses. The identity shifts to the soul itself, and we are free to explore the world of mythology and energy as a participant and influencer.

This may sound like science fiction or like the story of a cliché "party drug" to many readers, yet this manner of experience is ancient and universal among human experiences. Like all the types of spiritual expe-rience, it is nearly impossible to impart the depth of the "reality" of these moments. This means that we really *feel* as if we are the Cosmic Self. The experience is believable and qualitatively as real as anything else we've known. Our self-awareness and style of thinking remains somewhat normal, while our perception of our abilities is different.

A friend of mine, Jerry, provides an excellent case study. I met Jerry at a spiritual group that I attend regularly. An easily likable, intelligent, and good-humored man, Jerry presents himself as "ordinary," but soon after the meeting began I learned otherwise. Once he felt safe among our friends Jerry confided in us about what was happening to him.

"It is crazy," he began, "It is as real as me sitting here talking with you, but it is happening while I am asleep. When I go to bed it is like I wake up *in* the dream. When I wake up in the dream I am as alert and aware as I am right now. The difference is that I have these amazing powers. I can think of a place and then I am transported there instantly. I am seeing and interacting with people and the place like they were real.

"I've had vivid dreams before, but this is different. It is as real as my waking life and I am fully conscious and choosing in each moment. Time bends, and I feel like I am away for a week. But, that's not all. I can travel to places that I have never even seen or heard of before. You guys have to understand, I have been a business man all my life. I was a senior accounts manager in the corporate office of one of the nation's leading banks! If they heard me talk about this they'd think I am crazy–I think I am crazy!

"I have been traveling in dimensions of light and sound and experiencing sacred beings and all this kind of stuff. What is going on? I have seriously been worried about my mental health.

"Now, here is the weird part. I started to receive information and see things in my lucid dreams that I would remember and write down when I got up in the morning. Finally, just a couple of weeks ago I started reading some books that spiritual counselors have recommended and I find that the things they are writing about I already know—I learned it in my dreams! I've never seen this stuff before and yet I am being told it in my dreams while I am flying around from place to place! I am actually getting information that is verifiable!"

Over time Jerry has learned to direct his dreaming and apply what he has been learning. He is experiencing another dimension to himself, and he has different abilities in that state. The gift of what he is seeing and learning is actually making sense. It is creating a radical transformation of his life and the way he understands the world. This is not a fantasy that Jerry is making up. The things he feels and knows now are consistent with generations of mystical teachings. Jerry journeys very much like the shamans of ancient times—and he didn't even know what a shaman is.

Of course Jerry is not physically flying all over the world at night, but it does seem that something more than fantasy is occurring in his awareness. Recently, Jerry called me to tell me that he actually met someone while in his cosmic self who recognized him. They then met in the physical world the next day and mutually confirmed the encounter. I know a number of people who have met and interacted in the dream time; it is not as uncommon as you might think.

The Cosmic Self and Healing

This may sound rather unbelievable to people from Western-minded societies and yet it is foundational to the worldview of Indigenous people. *Chivengwa*, my Venda African teacher in South Africa frequently dreams about his patients before they come to see him. In the dreams he will learn what is wrong and the most effective way to treat it. I have seen this in action and know for certain this is not a mere story.

Another African healer whom I have become close with is *Mandaza*, a Shona healer from Zimbabwe. Sometimes he travels into his Cosmic Self while awake. Countless times we have seen him sitting with patients, he closes his eyes and at will he is able to travel to places within his patients' life, even within their body. This remarkable gift is not uncommon among Indigenous healers. It is a useful state of consciousness in which information may be accessed about the world and how to create a healing effect in it. Traveling in the Cosmic Self is natural to shamans of all cultures and ages.

I recall an amusing time when I was visiting with an *Anishinabe* (Ojibway) traditional healer friend of mine out on a reservation north of Winnipeg. Tom is one of the most gifted and powerful healers I have ever known. Having studied the ceremonies, herbs, and states of consciousness that heal since he was a child, Tom was known to some as "the Elder's Elder." Revered among healers, Tom kept mostly to himself and often withdrew from social settings to protect his energy and manage his constant access to "psychic information."

One day when I went up to see him on the reservation, Tom asked me, "Have you ever seen a guy with a big afro and a bright orange dress?" I laughed out loud. I thought he was making a joke, since Tom was rarely serious when we visited. Suddenly, I got an image in my mind of the Hindu guru "Sai Baba." Sai Baba wears orange robes, and has a large ball of frizzy hair atop his head.

"Oh, wait. Maybe I do know someone like that. Can you tell me more?" My skeptical side always wanted to test these things out. "Sure. He has a big afro, but he is not African or African-American. I don't know where he is from, but he's not black. His skin color is like mine," Tom said. "He has lots and lots of people that seem to support him, or follow him. I mean *lots*. And he has a white chariot with white horses. Maybe it's a car or something, but I see it as a white chariot."

"Okay, okay," I interrupted, "I do know who that is. His name is Sai Baba. He looks just like you described and he is famous (or infamous) for his fleet of fancy cars. You could say they are his chariots—BMW, Mercedes, and in particular he was known for a white long stretch limo!"

"Well! You can tell him to stop visiting me. He travels in his 'astral body' to check on me, I think he wants to know how I do my work. Unless he asks properly, he can buzz off!"

"How bizarre," I thought, "two masters of the Cosmic Self meeting in the dream-time each aware of the other and acting out as if awake!" I could hardly imagine. Eventually, I got used to this reality. Though I only experience it from time to time, many of the spiritual healers I have worked with have visited me in my dreams, and they find it a normal experience.

Once when in the midst of a vision quest in South Dakota I fell asleep midday and had a dream of a badger coming into my circle and walking closely past me. I woke up suddenly and was unsure if it had happened or not. When I got home to Manitoba I visited Tom, the *Anishinabe* healer who was running a traditional medicine clinic for the reservation nursing station. Between patients I went into the room where he was working to sit and talk. I sat down, and saw that he had set up a sacred space, an altar, with his objects of healing and power. It was all set out on a badger skin and my eyes must have widened in surprise. I wondered if it was he who came to visit me in my questing site. As if he heard my question, Tom answered, "Didn't you see me? I came to check on you."

When I worked in healthcare settings I met a number of people who confided in me that they attributed their healing to events and healing encounters that took place in lucid dreams or due to astral journeys of the self beyond the body. Some of them received guidance about the medicine they should or should not take. Others experienced healing themselves or others through energy and light in a dissociated state, sometimes while awake, sometimes while dreaming. Some experienced themselves actually extracting illness and "negative energy" from their body. Naturally, they did not tell their medical doctors, nor did I, for these were "normal" emotionally and socially well-adjusted people, who just happened to be blessed with the grace of an experience of the Cosmic Self.

Medically Induced

I once met a woman named Susan who was in a terrible car accident. Her life was picture perfect until that moment. It was perfect to everyone but Susan. She described to me how she had become extremely successful in her career, popular among friends, loved by family, and yet somehow disconnected from her sense of meaning and purpose in life. She had thought about making a change, but life's momentum and the expectations of others always took precedent.

One day on her way home from work she was in a terrible accident. Just as a large semitrailer was passing her in the opposite direction, a small sports car darted out from behind it, directly into her lane. In what she describes as less than an instant, she was in a high speed, head-on collision. Both cars were demolished; the other driver was killed instantly. Susan was found already in a coma and was taken to the hospital where she was put on life support.

Susan recalls a number of dreamlike memories. Dreams of family. Dreams of strange worlds and moving lights and colors. Most significantly and vividly, however, she recalled a time when she watched herself lying in the hospital bed, as if she were a fly on the wall. She watched a few friends come and go that day, saw the nurse check on her from time to time, and mostly was aware of how alone she was. At one point two medical residents came in to discuss her case.

They came in laughing. One man was talking to the other about his relationship with a woman he was thinking of asking to marry him. It was obvious he had "cold feet" and was beginning to review all the things that might go wrong. The conversation turned to sarcastic humor as he began to bolster his own self by belittling this woman he reported to be in love with.

Susan recalled this with frustration. "He was obviously in love, obviously happy. But he was looking for excuses to get out of the relationship. He was just afraid of getting hurt. I tried to tell him not to make that mistake. I had become successful in material ways, but I never let anyone into my life. I couldn't bear watching someone else make that same mistake. I called to him to get his attention. I yelled and yelled—but he couldn't hear me."

The two interns finished their conversation and checked the equipment and vital signs they had come to record. They paused and looked at Susan. "It is sad," one said to the other. "I don't think this will end well. Let's just hope it ends soon." Susan was horrified as she recounted the moment. "Then, I lost the memory. The next thing I recall is waking up. Soreness, dry mouth, and the room seemed so bright."

A day later as I began to stay awake for longer periods of time, one of the residents came in—the one who was going to get engaged. "Welcome back Susan, we were worried about you, but it looks like everything will be okay. You are a very lucky woman."

Susan replied to the young doctor, "You said I was going to die. You didn't think I'd make it." Shocked, he replied, "No, I would never say that. Dr. Johnson was the one who was very—wait, what makes you say that? Did someone tell you that he said that?" Susan replied, "I heard him, he thought I'd die. And you, you were running from your girlfriend! How could you? You were the one who wanted to marry her."

The intern turned white as a hospital sheet. Susan said he looked like he was about to cry. "I don't understand, I never told anyone, except Dr. Johnson. Tim and I are close friends. He is going to be my best man." "You mean, you are getting married?" Susan asked with growing energy. "Yes, we've been engaged for over a month now. We'll be married in six months from this weekend."

He paused, and softened his voice, "It is true, I was having doubts and I acted like an idiot looking for ways out. But something told me not to let that happen. It was like a voice that haunted me for days. It was my conscience I guess. I am glad I listened, my fiancé is amazing. Dr. Johnson on the other hand is a loud mouth and I am sorry he spoke to you about this today. It is your first day back in two months—you don't need to hear about my love life." Susan tried to explain, "You don't understand, I heard *you*."

"You are sweet, Susan, but you have been in a severe coma, and I know that the day Dr. Johnson and I were in here together was weeks ago. I would not have spoken casually if you had the physical capacity to hear us. You don't need to protect him. We go way back. Now, you rest up, you're just a bit confused."

Susan knew then that what she had read about in books and magazines was true. People really do have consciousness outside their bodies. She had an out-of-body experience. This was extraordinary and yet somehow it seemed totally natural. Since that day Susan has changed her life in the most amazing ways. She is dedicated to a meditation practice, she has changed her career to one that makes a difference in the world, she is dating more, and she is in the best physical health of her life. "I've been given a gift. We all have—it's life. I am not about to waste it."

It is ironic that the Cosmic Self has no place in Western medicine or psychology, and yet medical emergencies and physical crises are a common source of experiences of the Cosmic Self. As with experiences of the Spirit World there are no good explanations for how or why these experiences occur, though there are thousands upon thousands of documented accounts of "out-of-body experiences," "near-death experiences," and "lucid dreams." Studies in neurology at best show that there are correlations between these experiences and changes in brain activity. Nothing scientific yet explains the meaning, accuracy, or reality of the encounters people have when experiencing the Cosmic Self.

When Do People Experience the Cosmic Self?

It is an unusual person who has the ability to intentionally create an experience of the Cosmic Self. Nevertheless, shamans, visionaries, and some spiritual teachers do have this ability. I have met many untrained, spiritually uneducated people who naturally experience out-of-body awareness, or lucid dreams on a regular basis. For most people such an experience comes unexpectedly. These experiences may occur through intention, or, more often, spontaneously during a spiritual practice, crisis, or without forewarning. There are no rules about where and when it may occur. The Cosmic Self is ever-waiting to be revealed. The Cosmic Self is ever-present, like the stars above us. Most of us only see them at night, and think that because we cannot see them in the bright light of day that they are no longer watching over us. In fact, they are. It is only perception that hides the stars and the Cosmic Self.

The reality of the Cosmic Self was once taken for granted by ancient healers. In the modern world it has slowly become concealed and rejected by science and fear. Science has rejected the Cosmic Self, doubting what cannot be measured. Religion has condemned the Cosmic Self in fear of the power of the individual to access mastery and influence over the physical world, and perhaps the fear that people may do harm through it. Because the Cosmic Self operates by non-ordinary senses and at a very subtle level of energy and consciousness, it may remain a mysterious and contested reality, unless individuals have the courage to acknowledge their experiences and share them more openly. As this happens, it will become clear how natural the Cosmic Self really is.

Experiences of the Cosmic Self may include:

- Out-of-Body Experiences
- Near-Death Experiences
- Lucid dreams (dreams in which we are awake and intentional in the dream state)
- Astral travel (dreamlike experiences, often while asleep or in deep meditation)
- The natural or developed ability to perceive and/or manipulate energy while in a state of experiencing the self *as* energy.
- Dreams and visions in which we share awareness with an animal or person.
- Past life regression experiences.

The Burden of Divine Senses

The Cosmic Self can be experienced in many ways and not all are easy or pleasant. As a young adult a great teacher of mine shared stories of the paralyzing pain of experiencing the emotional heart of the Cosmic Self. Wildly empathic, the Cosmic Self in this woman became awakened to the suffering of the world in such a personal and intimate way that it literally made her sick with grief. In the boundless and limitless capacity of the Cosmic Self, she became so astutely aware of the suffering of others, that it was as if she could hear the inner cries of every soul in pain. This experience, she reports, not only awakened the depth of her compassion, but it nearly cost her the job she had and her health. I have known a number of people to have experienced this and similar aspects of the Cosmic Self that were so intense that the experiences overwhelmed their psychological and physical ability to cope.

I recall one such time while I was driving on a beautiful mountain road, listening to a piece of music that I had never heard before. It was wonderful and deeply moving. It began like a moment of Truth and Beauty. I felt the perfection of the moment, the beauty of the singer, and the majesty of the natural world. Slowly, the experience shifted to a moment of Ordinary Magic in which the very twists and turns in the melody seemed orchestrated to the rises and falls in the road.

Every passing hawk, or glimpse of a sweeping view seemed as if planned, synchronized with the words, the intensity, and flow of the music. Thoughts about the natural world to unlock the power of The Sacred came to me, and seconds later the song echoed the exact sentiments. I could not have coordinated the moment better had I all the time and talent in the world.

Without anticipation or warning my perception shifted into the realm of the Cosmic Self.

I felt as if I was more spirit than human, more soul than matter. My hands on the wheel seemed disconnected. I heard the singer and saw her, images of her life, and the love and pain she felt that gave birth to the song. I began to cry.

Pulling over to the side of the road, I closed my eyes in empathic grief. The trees began to share their stories; the wind and stones also. It was as if I could hear the emotional history of the land. There was an ancient legacy, old as time, and a deep, deep, sense of loss. Forests here had been clear cut, the land excavated for resources, and the air itself now polluted; a haze could be seen over nearby towns and cities from the mountainside.

The sorrow was unlike anything I had known. Literally, my body was clenched in a torturing ache, as if my own child had been taken or harmed. It was in intense physical pain. I wept and wept uncontrollably at the sadness of the land, the loss of the relations and relatives. Generations cut down without respect or honoring. The creatures, plants, waterways, and the earth itself shared a sense of loss with me that pushed me to the edge of my capacity to think and feel.

I don't share this story often, for many see it as a psychological projection and dismiss it. Over the years, however, I have met many healers, teachers, and common people, who have had such an experience. As if they encountered a spiritual dimension to their heart and had an enhanced capacity for empathy and feeling. In the Indigenous world, shamans and healers take such an experience very seriously and have long recognized the ability of the human being to "hear," "see," and "feel," from the Cosmic Self. In ancient traditions, it was how we knew to be in relationship to the world: we let the world teach us directly. We trusted our spiritual senses and knew we were relatives of all things. Through this interconnection we can, in some spiritual states, feel things, know things, and see things beyond our own experience.

Unlimited You

When we experience the Cosmic Self, there is a natural capacity and even a tendency to overlap and merge into other spiritual dimensions and levels of experience. Experiences of the Cosmic Self may trigger a moment of Truth and Beauty, they may lead us to participatory encounters of the Spirit World, or they may even allow us to create situations that others might experience as Ordinary Magic. What defines the experience of the Cosmic Self is the self-awareness of a personal power to move within the Spirit World and the world of Divine Energy itself. Rather than simply witnessing the Spirit World, we are able to interact and direct outcomes. In the experience of the Cosmic Self we become participants, not just observers, in the spiritual world. These experiences awaken us to the reality that consciousness and awareness is the foundational field of life, and that we, in truth are spiritual beings. We are more soul and spirit, than flesh and bone. We discover that we are first and foremost a being of tremendous power and wisdom. The Cosmic Self reveals that our bodies and five senses provide us with a wonderful but limited perception of the world.

Exercise

Exercises with the Cosmic Self are complex to teach through a book. I highly recommend seeking guidance and a facilitated experience by a hypnotherapist, a shamanic journey guide, past life regressionist, or a skilled facilitator of guided imagery. You may also look up guided imagery sessions on digital audio or online. I recommend sessions at least 30 minutes in length to increase your chance of truly surrendering and making the leap from imagination to Cosmic Self. A one hour session is ideal.

Chapter Six

The Experience of Divine Energy

When we experience this Sacred Force we
know that all things are connected,
emerging from and fueled by the same energy and source.
This force is not personal, yet it responds to thought and emotion.
It carries intelligence, feels like love and moves
in complex and clear pathways and patterns.
In such moments we understand the web of energy
and life force that governs creation.
If we know how to look, we see that at all levels of existence
we are only a dance of
energy and consciousness.

When the Darkness Becomes the Light

Sleep was difficult that first night in the Amazon jungle. Though the cabin I slept in was mostly screened windows, the night covered us in an impenetrable darkness. The tall canopy of giant leaves and lush vines robbed the forest floor of any light from the midnight sky of stars. The heat felt like a thick, damp blanket covering and absorbing everything. I felt heavy and lay motionless, sweating in the fever of the tropical night. Though my body felt debilitated by the heat and darkness, my mind was awake and aware of the living world around us.

A symphony of insects, frogs, and night birds echoed and resonated in all directions. Sharp whistles, deep humming, sporadic cackles, and the sounds of tiny buzzing wings filled the blackness. Just as sleep crept into my room, something else called to me from the jungle. Every moment: a new sound, a new scent, the roar of Howler monkeys, was like a roll of thunder moving through the trees. Laying there awake was more dreamlike than any dream I had known. It was a dream come true.

When I set foot on the soil of the Amazon River banks, I felt like I had returned to a long lost home. I had always wanted to travel to the Amazon River. The desire began when I was young, only six years old. At night before bed I would explore the natural history encyclopaedias that were kept in my room. The jungle's dark green world of brilliant birds, ancient waterways, and silent jaguars called me. It felt like a part of myself I had left behind—or had yet to remember.

I wished I could be transported on the back of a jaguar to the warm banks of the Amazon. I prayed for some magical force to unite me with this wondrous creature I had seen in books and on television. If only I wished it enough, it felt like it might come true. It is difficult to describe the sense of connection and longing a person can have for a place—as if it were necessary to the fulfilment of their soul. Many years later, I understood that fulfilment in a journey on that great river.

Through a truly bizarre set of coincidences and synchronicities, that can only be described as Ordinary Magic, I found an opportunity to travel to the Amazon over an extended spring break during college. I went as a volunteer with an incredible medical expedition team called Amazon Promise. Amazon Promise, then and now, takes Western medical supplies, doctors, nurses, traditional healers, and an ethnobotanist to remote villages that have no access to Western care.

The problem these Indigenous river-people face is not only the lack of Western care, but the cultural devastation left by the missionary groups who convinced them that their traditional herbal and spiritual remedies were ineffective and evil. Having lost faith in their own culture, the people are now falling ill and even dying from simple conditions that can be cured with the plants growing underneath their thatched homes. The trip lasted more than a month and was more incredible that I could have imagined. Things I saw, shared and learned will be with me all my life.

At the beginning of our trip we visited the jungle camp of a group of three shamans. Shamans are masters of the Cosmic Self and possess a deep relationship to the Spirit World. One, who spoke English, has since transformed their small family camp into a cultural center. There we stayed to receive teachings about local culture, plants, and healing practices. On the last night of our stay with the shamans, a special healing ceremony was held. We were allowed to watch and pray with the visionary healers, but not to participate fully, since this was a medical team with a service orientation. They did not want to endorse any particular shaman or practice, nor expect the volunteers to feel comfortable doing so.

We all gathered after dusk beneath a thatched hut roof, benches wrapped around the sides facing inward, but there were no walls. There was only jungle all around and the growing darkness. The ceremony began with a spiritual cleansing of each member of our team and then we took our seats around the sacred outdoor temple. The shamans sat at the front behind a long table that was an altar of sacred objects and medicines. They became increasingly distant, as if far off in another world, as they sang their healing songs and smoked big black tobacco cigarettes.

They chanted and prayed long into the night. Their *shakapa* rattles, made of dried bundles of leaves, infused the space with a soft, yet steady and rapid rhythm. The songs and sounds ebbed and flowed like waves on a shore, steady and entrancing. Despite the magic of the setting it was getting late and one by one our team grew tired and left.

We entered the depth of the night and still the three men sat chanting, smoking, shaking their *shakapas* and praying. It seemed like it would never end. I had been in ceremonies that were similar to this in Indigenous American communities, and felt committed to maintain my focus and endurance. Ceremonies like the Lakota "*Lowanpi*," and "*Yuwipi*," and the Cree "*Shaking Tent*," were similar in some ways. They lasted all night as the shamans traveled through experiences of the Cosmic Self into other realms of the Spirit World to acquire information to heal and help patients and their communities.

I prayed and meditated with these weathered healers, determined to last through the night if need be. I felt that if I could just stay focused on projecting my soul, my intention into their field of awareness, that somehow I could be "in" the spirit world with them. I had experienced the Cosmic Self before, and knew that I could use my intention and imagination to engage it. "If it is real, then they'd know," I thought.

At one point, I closed my eyes and something changed. At first I thought I was falling asleep. My awareness of my body and my own thoughts dissolved into an awareness of a dim flickering light in the darkness of my inner vision. I felt like something was shining from the shamans' songs toward me.

The darkness was vast and everywhere and everything, except for the flickering light that had my attention. I was no longer aware of myself in any way at all. It was as if I had dissolved into the darkness. I became the empty, infinite space and the flickering light was within me. Slowly, the space I had become a part of began to flex and flow, as if it had depth and texture. Soon the fluid emptiness revealed its dimensions as the flickering light grew into a haze of fiery colors—yellow, orange, red. I lost any sense of self-awareness: I was oblivious to temperature, external sounds, sensations, and even the feeling of my own body.

The colors danced and sparkled as one massive, endless field of light. It was as if my awareness was swimming in a sea of pure light and energy. I had no sense of myself as a traveler, no sense of "me" exploring the energy, I *was* the energy, and a nameless awareness moving within it. The expansiveness of the feeling extended and extended, and although I had lost any sense of having a body or an identity, I remained alert within a pure awareness. The awareness was observing something unfolding. This was not a formless world, nor was I aware of a Cosmic Self. There were no spirits, no voices, no magical thoughts or talents. This was different and very strange at first. I was an ocean of energy, and the currents moved, surged, and flowed without my direction or participation. All I could do was surrender.

Suddenly my awareness was confined within the tiniest particle of light within the swirling, surging sea of energy and I felt the ability to travel through the field of light, the sea of energy. I was the sea, and a drop of water in it. I was not human or aware of any human quality. I had become a particle or a wave of energy.

I could travel in an instant to any place within the field of energy, which was everyplace. The colors shifted and moved. I felt as if I had entered the subatomic dimension of existence. This is a dimension in which everything exists in a unified field of energy, a matrix of life force. Einstein and many great physicists, such as David Bohm Ph.D., Niels Bohr Ph.D., and Arthur Eddington Ph.D., saw this subtle field of energy as the very foundation of reality itself. Deepak Chopra has called it the "sub-manifest order of being." It is not tangible, and yet it is the superstructure of potential and design that all things flow out of.

I explored this field of energy with the subtlest sense of will and curiosity. As a particle of energy, I could see the level of reality in which miracles made sense, clairvoyance was logical, energy healing was natural, and the magic gifts of the yogis and shamans were easily explained. Experiences of Ordinary Magic, the Spirit World, and even the Cosmic Self, all made sense. The mechanics felt clear and obvious: the created world arises from a field of pure energy that is both intelligent and unlimited in potential. The intelligence is reflected in its innate structure and responsiveness; its potential is expressed through its freedom from time, space, and the permanence of any form.

When we experience the Divine Energy, we see at the most elemental level who and what we are: energy and awareness. We are consciousness itself.

This light, which physicists may call the quantum field, others may call "spirit." However you describe this foundation of existence, its nature lays at the edge of reason. The mind can scarcely grasp it, though in moments of Divine Energy, we see it, feel it, and become it. Like an infinite ocean in all directions, it is one substance which takes shape through waves, currents, and layers of depth and complexity. As patterns and designs become repeated, energy moves into form.

When patterns and designs are destroyed or broken, energy is released and returned to potential. We experience this phenomena even when we break habits, change jobs, or fall in love. We are as waves that crest and fall in this great sea. Each aspect of self that comes and goes is but a ripple upon the wave that is our life. Each wave is eventually returned to the ocean. The ocean is the field of Divine Energy, and because that ocean is intelligent and aware, we recognize it as consciousness. In that moment of shifting light and loss of self, this was more than an idea, but a direct perception of the space where mind and matter converge.

It was simply a matter of focusing awareness. If I had the slightest shift in focus or awareness the energy field would change. I did not feel as if I was in a dimension of reality and that The Spiritual World or God was separate from the world, rather I had the distinct awareness in the moment that this was the hidden dimension of reality that *is the world*, and everything we do not see in between. It is the world that the shamans and energy healers are masters of and of which modern physicists are students.

I had no self-awareness of my body or mental chatter. I was conscious of my thoughts, but only as they arose. At that level of being, intention and volition could coexist with total interconnectedness. Time and space were not present, and yet pattern and design were implied. Intention and feeling were the conductors within the matrix; they were the operating principle between this sub-manifest world of energy and the physical world itself.

As I settled my mind from its excitement at the infinite possibilities that might be found through learning to manipulate the world of energy and power, a sudden shift occurred. All the rhythms of the energy that created the sensation of traveling, moving beyond time and space, broke away into a still point. A moment in which the only feeling that was present was love. This was a prelude to the next experience of The Sacred that we will discuss in the following chapter: Formless Spirit.

Awareness shifted, and energy gave way to a simpler more essential level and it was love. I *was* love. Nothing else existed but the energy and sensation of pure, flowing unconditional love—no mind, no body, no will or intention. Only love, radiant and shining.

Soon, I began to regain my sense of physical form. I felt the flow of energy now coming from a direction—from above. I sat as if in a ray of sunlight, pure bliss, joy, flowing from an invisible source into me—body, mind, and spirit. I was like a small cup in a waterfall; the force was vigorous and enlivening. It was overwhelming, and infinitely abundant. As I slowly came to my senses, all I could do in that moment was pray to receive that love, to infuse my life with it and to share it. My only response was not so much a thought as a deep guttural feeling: "gratitude!"

Finally, exhausted, the sounds of the jungle creatures crept into my awareness, and I became fully alert to my body. I looked up and the shamans were finishing the ceremony. A candle was now lit and they had stopped singing. A voice in the shadows said, "*buenos sueños*", which means "good dreams." Sometimes it is used to say goodnight. I took my cue, got up, and wandered blissfully back to the little cabin where I slept.

In the morning when I stepped outside the cabin, one of the shamans came rushing over to me. "Last night," he said "you stay with us. We see you." He made a gesture with his hands as if showing a bird flying from his chest. "We *see* you." He paused and looked me in the eye, "We want to make ceremony with you. When can you come back?"

I was surprised by the invitation and by the success of the ceremony and my intention. It seemed that as he saw both the Spirit World and the Divine Energy, somehow they knew what I had experienced. He even described watching my soul take flight. I was convinced, but astounded. At the end of my tour with the medical team, four weeks later, I returned alone to visit those shamans and spent a life-changing week learning about the medicine of the Amazon and experiencing the ceremonies of the jungle.

The Field of Infinite Light

In the experience of Divine Energy you directly experience the subtle world of energy and spirit that lies within and around the world of form. Here you will encounter truly original and unexpected phenomena, as well as a profound sense of interrelationship between the microcosmic and macrocosmic levels of reality. Out on the edge of the quantum physical and astrophysical worlds we discover spiritual truths that redefine our understanding of the world. At this level of experience and perception, science and spirit converge. There we find universes within universes. These dimensions are experienced through levels of sensation, image, and intuition that are impossible to fully describe.

There are a few hallmarks of this type of spiritual experience. First, body awareness typically vanishes completely and there is a general loss of self-awareness. The ego dissolves and merges with that which you are seeing or sensing. This is not a conceptual experience or a sudden realization of ideas. This is a *direct* experience, and almost never occurs in ordinary moments or during everyday activities.

The experience of Divine Energy has both a transcendent and physical quality. It is often communicated through the language of science and art. During such experiences one feels as if the body has shut down and perception becomes passive. Most people feel as if they are being "shown" something, as opposed to the feeling of having control or conscious will.

Experiences of Divine Energy are fundamentally experiences of light and color with pattern and meaning. Divine Energy is the inspiration for modern expressions like fractal art, quantum theory, psychedelic design and "tie-dye" art. There are also many accounts of Divine Energy in the shamanic and visionary stories, writings, and ancient art of the past.

Divine Energy is much more than a hallucination, or psychedelic daydream. Indeed, the Indigenous traditions of Sacred Plant Medicine, from Peyote to Maria Sabina's Divine Mushrooms, are well known for helping people to access this realm of Knowing and Vision. I would not classify such encounters as hallucinations. The content of experiences of Divine Energy is profoundly significant and typically has a lasting impact on the worldview of the person who experiences it. When we examine written accounts of Divine Energy we find striking parallels in the fields of physics, chemistry, and microbiology. Many who have experienced Divine Energy, describe a fluid and amorphous quality of energy, light, and color. In the same breath, they speak of patterns, designs, and currents of light and energy that corroborate and align with explanations of energy medicine, mind–body practices and modern physics. Often, experiences of Divine Energy feel like direct perceptions of the atomic and sub-atomic levels of the world.

You Can't Get There from Here

The experience of Divine Energy is typically encountered during or through:

- Deep meditation
- Spontaneously during a guided shamanic journey
- Holotropic breathwork
- Advanced yogic breathing techniques
- Deep trance states induced through movement, art, sound and/or breathwork
- The use of Indigenous plant medicines (in ceremonial settings and under experienced supervision)
- Spontaneously through grace and any steady or intense spiritual practice with a physical element such as Advanced Pranayama, Sexual Tantric practices, or even some intense forms of yoga that typically have a long duration and intense mind–body elements.

The Subatomic Secret of Life

In my experience and study I have noticed a correlation between practices that tend to be extreme in physical nature and the occurrence of these states. There are some people who seem to naturally access this sort of awareness, however, of all seven territories of the spirit, it appears to be the least commonly discussed in our spiritual traditions. Accounts and images of light, color, and sound are certainly common. The totally absorbed experience of Divine Energy, on the other hand, occurs far less in ancient texts.

It is possible that such accounts are rare because past cultures had no language, medium, or metaphor to explain what they were seeing. In modern times the advent of science, technology based art and a focus on non-personal (formless) ideas of God and The Sacred have allowed people to speak more easily of these experiences. Another explanation is that these experiences are simply less common. Regardless of how common or uncommon, experiences of Divine Energy are universal, pervasive, and important to learn from.

Modern spiritual seekers and teachers have begun to envision and account for the world of Divine Energy, many without the direct experience. Through inference, science, intuition, and other spiritual states, the world of Divine Energy naturally begins to become evident. There is a growing movement of spiritual science and science-based spirituality lead by authors and teachers like Gregg Braden, Ken Wilber, Candice Pert Ph.D., John Hagelen Ph.D., Dean Radin Ph.D., Lynn McTaggert, Fred Alan Wolf Ph.D., William Tiller, Ph.D., Gary Schwartz Ph.D., and Stewart Hameroff M.D. At the heart of the philosophy and science of these great thinkers is the understanding that the world is entirely comprised of Divine Energy.

The popular films "What The (bleep) Do We Know" and its revised format, "Further Down the Rabbit Hole," explore the science, philosophy, psychology and spirituality of modern physics and neurology. These popular concepts of the universe and the nature of the soul were well described years ago in a very accessible book by Larry Dossey, M.D., called *Rediscovering the Soul*. In it, he simplifies much of quantum physics to help create scientific foundation for understanding consciousness, non-local awareness, and the phenomena of the soul.

Though not always directly experienced, Divine Energy provides a believable, practical, and inspiring concept of The Sacred for many people today. Many who have been raised in a scientistic world find it reasonable to recognize that "God" is in fact "The Universe" and that "The Universe" is in fact comprised entirely of energy—subtle, all pervasive, intelligent, and multidimensional.

How to Enter the Light

In my research, training, and experience I have found no easy way to guarantee the experience of Divine Light. This and the following two categories of experience seem to rest very much upon "grace"—the spontaneous touch of The Sacred. You might also say that the constellation of factors that create or lead to such experiences are not at all well understood or known. Also, unlike the first four types of spiritual experience, ability, skill, and aptitude have little to do with entering the Divine Energy. Because there is no self, ego, or body awareness during a true experience of Divine Energy, choosing or controlling is contradictory to its nature. A critical and essential key, however, is the capacity to surrender all will and attachment with a deep openness to experience without control or knowing what is next.

Naturally, there are always exceptions.

While discussing Divine Energy in a small group lecture one day a very unassuming woman in her early fifties put her hand up. "Just a few weeks ago, I was jogging on the beach in the Los Angeles area. I could feel myself entering a very focused state and my thoughts had slipped away. There was nothing but the beauty of the day, the freedom of my body and the freshness of the wind off the ocean. I have no idea how to explain this, but I was suddenly out of my body, or I forgot my body. I was a tiny particle in the air. It was like my awareness jumped into an atom of air—whatever that means. I was floating, then racing through the jet stream. I could feel, see, and understand the way the wind moved, though I "saw" nothing. I was not aware of myself observing it. Then, as I raced through the sky and into the cosmos, I thought, 'Wow, this is so amazing!' In that moment, I was 'back in my body' running on the beach. Was that an experience of Divine Energy?"

After having described how rare it is to experience Divine Energy, I was surprised, though thrilled to agree, "Yes, I do believe that was!"

Then, a young man put his hand up. "I am a med student just beginning my residency, and I think I had an experience like that as well."

"Really?" I was now shocked at the unfolding number of stories in a group of only ten or so. "Can you tell us what it was like?"

"Well, it actually seems impossible to explain, and I am sure my professors would think I am crazy. Since they aren't here, I guess I'll tell you. I had just come home from a marathon shift. I am pretty sure I worked about 40 hours straight, with very little sleep—just a few naps. I was exhausted, but unable to sleep when I got home, so I thought I'd try to study. That often makes me tired.

I was reviewing my hematology text, studying something about abnormal red blood cells. I recall that I fell into a bit of a trance. I was staring at the page, not asleep, but not awake. The next thing I knew *I was a red blood cell*! It was totally weird and totally amazing. I was racing through veins, capillaries, webs and networks of vascular (circulatory) system. I was nothing but a speeding awareness. Everything made sense: the webs, the patterns, the functions. I even saw cells replicating. My awareness got smaller and smaller until I felt like an impulse of electricity.

I don't think I had a thought at that moment, but somehow knew I was a wave of light or electricity traveling through the nervous system. I ended up in the brain, and then into a perception of energy in which I saw the whole body as a field of light. I was seeing the heart of every atom, at the heart of every cell—and all there was, was light! In that moment I spontaneously thought, 'anything can be healed: the body is fluid. It can be formed by the mind's will over the energy of its structure." He paused, and looked at us all with his own shock. "Of course, I am not even sure if I believe what I just said!" He laughed.

"What the heck does that mean!?" he concluded. "I don't know if that counts as one of your Divine Energy experiences." The group sat in quiet awe. I smiled, "Yes, that gets a passing grade."

You Are the Light

The experience of Divine Energy is by its very nature mysterious and sacred. Regardless of a person's belief going into the experience, what it reveals feels precious, important, accurate and very real. Whether we look at Divine Energy through the lens of science and philosophy, or just through the experience available to us, we encounter a radically valuable and ancient perspective on life. In these moments we become aware that at the smallest and subtlest level of creation is a force that's like energy, like a field of light. This force is what breathes in the nucleus of an atom; it is the essential building block of all things, growing and inert.

When we experience this Sacred Force we *know* that all things are connected, emerging from and fueled by the same source. This force is not necessarily personal, yet it has design, and laws that it tends towards. It responds to thought and emotion. It carries intelligence, feels like love, and moves in complex and clear pathways and patterns. In such moments we realize that we are the Divine Light and that Light is consciousness.

If we know how to look, we see that at all levels of existence we are only energy and consciousness at play. From this place, the judging mind and separation that we often foster in moments of worry, stress, and fear become absurd. If all people, places, and events are just different currents in one sea of life, how then do we condemn one or disown another. We recognize the responsibility of *relationship* and the influence of the mind and intent. When we realize that we are energy beings, we understand that our thoughts are prayers, our bodies are sacred, and every act is an act of power. Being intentional and compassionate becomes more than a good idea. It begins to feel absolutely necessary.

Chapter Seven

The Experience of the Formless Spirit

*Many spiritual experiences teach us about life,
about our world, and about ourselves.
The Formless Spirit teaches us that there is a dimension to existence
that is far beyond the created world and any form or duality.
In this experience we encounter eternity, infinity
and an essence that can only be called Love.
The Formless Spirit humbles the ego and silences the
mind, pointing us beyond the origins of the world.*

Death of Awareness, Birth of Spirit

The city of *Varanasi*, India, also known as *Benares*, has been a renowned holy city of pilgrimage for thousands of years, and that is what drew me there years ago. The chance to fulfil an ancient contract to pray by the waters of the great River Ganges had haunted me since I first read the Upanishads as a young teenager.

Much of the religious and spiritual activities in *Varanasi* focus on the great Ganges river. The sacred "*Ganga*" is a divine feminine force, a Goddess to many. The water has the power to cleanse the spiritual body: removing sin, healing illness and bestowing blessings. Many of the ancient scriptures describe how the Ganges carries the blessings from the feet of Lord Vishnu. This is why some call this sacred river, "*Vishnupadi*" which means, "Emanating from the Lotus feet of the Supreme Lord Vishnu." Throughout my travels in northern India it was difficult to lose awareness of Mother *Ganga*, for it seemed that so many sacred sites and pilgrim paths were known in relationship to the river. She is the guiding light and sustainer of many paths and practices.

While staying in *Varanasi* I used to spend the better part of my days wandering the banks of the Great Mother. At the edge of *Ganga* were temples, guest houses, and *ghats*—wide carved stone steps leading down into the water. Her banks were teaming with life and rituals. Wandering holy men, *Sadhus*, chanted and taught; individuals and families came to pray; and in certain designated areas were the "burning *ghats*." The burning *ghats* are where the bodies of the deceased are carefully brought, prepared, and ceremonially cremated in an open fire. The remaining ashes are released into the embrace of the Holy Mother; they are poured into the river. To be burned at the holy *ghats* by the Ganges is a prayer to be released from the cycles of birth and death. It liberates the soul.

For a short time in my life I trained and worked as a palliative care (end of life) spiritual counselor, and I had spent many hours with people who were dying. Once I overcame my original fear and discomfort, I learned to find the transition to be astonishingly beautiful. When the heart is open in the presence of death there is an implicit connection to the divine cycle and spirit of creation. In the presence of death I feel the loving energy of a Higher Power very near and in each moment.

I have found that it is only the human reactions of fear, attachment, and the desire to control life that creates suffering in the transitions within and from this world. When my dad died at age sixty-seven, I was in my early twenties and the loss was terrible and full of sorrow. Though I still miss him today, I can also say that the process was a miracle to be a part of. It was one of the most precious times in my life, and the sweetest time that he and I shared. Through death, I have learned so much about life, and so I was naturally attracted to the burning *ghats* and spent a lot of time at *Manikarnika*, one of the most revered and popular cremation sites.

One day in Varanasi I arrived at the end of a cremation ceremony. The family, dressed in beautiful colors and cuts of clothing, was preparing to leave the area. As they left, I settled into a place to meditate and pray on top of a low temple wall that bordered the area. I made myself comfortable as I planned to rest there awhile. I closed my eyes, and took a deep breath. I could smell the strangely comforting and almost sweet smoldering scent of burnt wood and floral offerings mixing with the unusual odour of human remains. Quickly, the scent of jasmine, then rose, and then some other incense overcame the harsh smell. Intoxicating fragrances from various homes, temples, and the nearby markets, were drifting in and adding to the enchantment. My eyes still closed, images of flowers blossomed in my inner vision while scenes from ancient ceremonies and sacred rites poured out in a kaleidoscope of color.

In the distance was the faint buzz and hum of rickshaws, mopeds, bells, and old diesel trucks. The vibration of life heightened my senses. A wave of sound poured over: human chatter, sacred chanting on a loud speaker somewhere, and dance music on a radio in a shop. Master of it all, the gentle song of the river whispered nearby as she washed the shore and played with the boats that crossed her expanse. Here there was no need for prayer or meditation. I only needed to open my senses—life was prayer, becoming absorbed in the drama was a meditation.

I realized that a new family was arriving with a body to cremate. Ritual attendants, and young assistants had been preparing a pier right before me and I had not noticed with my eyes closed and my senses so absorbed. The priest led the way as helpers and family followed. The body was carried on a narrow wooden platform, well wrapped in beautiful white fabric and modestly draped with flowers. The women followed like a rainbow of color and cloth. I watched the entire ceremony that day, maybe the only time I had seen one from the beginning to the end.

It seemed like a long process, and much of the afternoon had passed. Toward the end of the process, in my recollection, most of the family had left, and the funeral pier was burning down in size and intensity. I could still discern certain body parts; in particular, a portion of the skull was visible to me. Strangely, I felt a mix of emotion, the unfamiliar sight, and a warm growing sense of peace. The simplicity of life was relieving. In the end, we are all fragile, the body returns to the earth, and our time is complete—no matter how long or short. I focused my attention on that vision, and held the fragility of life in my heart and my mind.

"This too is me," I thought. "We'll all pass in time. The body is a vehicle for all that we truly are: spirit and soul. The only fear we feel in facing death arises when we cling to the illusion that this life has any permanence. We become attached and addicted to the stories and meaning we have created in our lives, and refuse to see the immense story that we are a part of. It is a story that never dies. The persona and the ego that we have identified with all our lives begins to diminish, and rather than embracing the brilliant eternity within, many grasp and cling to the past.

Cut off from a connection to a greater power, cut off from God, The Sacred, and the Divine Energy of the world, fear and a resistance to death naturally emerges. For death steals away all that we think we possess. In truth, our life is tremendously meaningful. Not because of anything we do, or any role we play. Life is meaningful because we are all a part of an infinite mystery, a sacred expression that unites us all. We are co-creators of this universe. We are all facets of The Sacred. We are all unique reflections of God. We are the shining facets of the only thing that exists. All waves, upon one ocean. There is not one moment when the wave is separate from its origin, only that it thinks it so. The crest and fall of a wave is not lost, but a return to its source and nature. So too are we expressions of the Sacred Origin of things. That fact alone is miraculous, amazing, and empowering.

There is nothing we need to do to be sacred or important—it is our natural condition. Death reveals the false things we become attached to. Death shows us what matters most. Death only brings us closer to the Source of All; it lifts the veil between us and the force that is our life and importance.

The thoughts subsided as I closed my eyes again and exhaled deeply. I do not remember my next breath.

In an instant, I lost myself. Unexpectedly and completely. It was as if I was swimming in a still pool. I released my breath and slipped below the surface. What remained was only a vast endless awareness, no self, no body, no time, no space, no object of attention. No thoughts. Just a deep open awareness. It had no subject, no edge, no patterns, or messages. There was only a presence, and a feeling. There was no separation between that presence and myself. There was no self and no self-awareness, only a subtle feeling. Looking back now I can say this experience was without form of any kind—no objects, images, or subjects. I had no will or intention, as I did in moments of Divine Energy. All senses and solidity to who "I am" vanished. Yet there was an overwhelming and distinct feeling in the awareness I had dissolved into: Love. Something within me remained conscious and aware, and this Love I was immersed in was more than limitless or unconditional. It was not a love "for" anything, since in that moment there was no "thing" to love. Love simply "was."

There at the edge of the burning *ghats*, the world dissolved into one dark expanse, with an endless and boundless feeling of what I can only call "creative force." It felt like love and joy infused with the power to create and destroy. It was like being blind in the depths of the ocean, but aware of the tide and currents. In this world, there is a vital impulse, a flowing force of change that emerges from the complete non-physical, unformed depths of The Sacred, and this too is God. This is the dimension of God that breathes at the edge of creation—call it what you like. This is a truth that lies beyond words; a place where the mind cannot enter. Even explaining it, cannot impart its truth.

Impossible as it may sound, this moment so empty of thought or self, carried a wisdom, a deeper glimpse into the depth and nature of The Sacred. Without ideas, I understood implicitly that all life, all rhythms, all matrixes of power and matter emerge from this realm of pure creative potential and imperceptible movement. Even the Divine Energy united and subtle in its features, is a circus of complexity and diversity in contrast to this moment of undifferentiated unity.

In such moments we see behind all levels of the created world and feel the vibration of the Creator Force. We enter a domain where only The Sacred, only God remains. This is not the place of "God," the discerning and wise being, this is God beyond form or energy. This is not the place of spirits or angels, this is not a place of things of any kind. There is no "this" or "that" in such a moment, yet it is immense and full, and feels like a Love that permeates all. Some might say that experiencing the Divine Energy is like knowing the mind of God. If so, then this moment of Formless Spirit is to know the heart of God.

The Formless Spirit has no features that can be grasped with the eye, or the mind. The heart remains the only manner of perception. Our identification with this dimension of God is so total and complete that the sense of self is immediately obliterated. There is a complete loss of ego, and concept of self. There is no body, mind, or awareness. Even the idea of "God" seems absurd: the convention, the limits, the concept, all fall short of what this experience reveals. Nevertheless, unlike the experience of Pure Consciousness, which we will explore next, there is a sense of "something" that is being merged with. There is still some awareness of consciousness itself—wordless, endless, edgeless, but with qualities and a sense of knowing.

The Formless Spirit is beyond death, before and within life; it is the creative impulse of the universe. In that moment I *was* the creative impulse and felt the cycle in which death and life dissolve into one. I was one with the Force of Life and knew it to be my origin, my innermost soul, and my destination. It is the Formless Spirit behind all things, giving endless birth, uniting all things in it.

The sound of children laughing and playing nearby suddenly pulled my awareness back to my body. I felt light-headed for a moment. I felt like a stone: slow, ancient, timeless. Each move was careful, as if the air were honey. My mind remained still. Not the least bit sleepy, I felt calm, as if I could sit for a thousand years.

The ordinary world reached for me, and I suddenly felt a sharp pain in my leg from sitting still so long in one place. The pain came as a surprise. Having a body seemed so odd. Was this really "my" body? Had I really worried so much about protecting it and wishing it to look well? Was I really confined to bones and blood, time and space? As I laughed at the foolishness of it all, my next breath came like a rush of wind. My next movement felt like my first ever. Truly, I was confined to a body! I felt a sorrow, and a great honor. Still dripping with the sweet vibration of Love and endless compassion, life called me back to its unfolding. Slowly, my senses returned and I found myself in India, sitting by the banks of the great river *Ganga*. The world in all its chaos and creativity floated by in peace, like flower petals upon the surface of the Great Mother Ganges.

A World beyond Worlds

Once touched by the Divine Heart, the Formless Spirit, it is difficult to embrace any teaching or path that leads to division or argues its own merit over any other. The Formless Spirit releases the fear of death, inspires the services of others, and inspires devotion to a life of kindness and connection. The experience of the Formless Spirit is the absolute affirmation of the omnipotence and omnipresence of The Sacred. It is at the core of all spiritual traditions and practices, and feeds the great mystical philosophies, teachings, and teachers. Traditions call it by different names: union, communion, revelation, samadhi, moksha, nirvana, heaven, salvation, and enlightenment; yet, all mystical paths converge on this experience.

Spiritual teachers, mystics, and healers throughout the ages have debated and differed in their perspectives about the role and importance of experiences of Divine Energy, the Cosmic Self, the Spirit World, and Ordinary Magic. The teachings and the experience of the Formless Spirit show little variation from culture to culture, era to era. Teachings of oneness, love, service, and self-identification with the Divine emerge from this state. It is important to realize that this experience informs and influences the lives of those who know it, yet it is not a state in which people reside. Few teachers throughout history have spent the majority of their lives in this state. Most spend their lives reflecting the brilliance of this state. They become and radiate, like the full moon that shows the light of a brighter truth we could not stand to look at directly.

When we enter the realm of Formless Spirit, we implicitly and *completely* lose our awareness of subject/object dimensions. I have experienced this state a number of times, and in all cases I felt physically debilitated and completely without the use of my mind or senses. I had no idea what was happening around me in any physical sense, and could only perceive a "level" of reality in which there is only oneness of power and presence. Great spiritual masters who are soaked in this consciousness and prone to return to this state with ease and spontaneity have needed to be cared for by followers and supporters. Unlike all the previously described experiences, the quality of perception is one in which we completely lose all self-awareness *and* subject awareness. You are no longer experiencing a thing outside yourself, you realize it is you and you are it. "It," still has qualities—such as bliss, love, union, peace—but it is not observed from the outside, it is known from a place of merging. Truly, if you haven't experienced it, it can be difficult to imagine, and for some, impossible to believe.

In the Formless Spirit, there is no separation between you and what you encounter. It is *not* the *realization* of oneness or the interrelationship of all things. It is the *experience* of only one thing: the source and force of all things. We experience The Sacred as eternal, infinite, and almost indescribable were it not for the qualities of love and spirit. In reviewing the writings of others who have experienced Formless Spirit it is difficult to discern if there are subtle differences in the feeling of the experience, or if the differences are merely reflective of the interpretations of the mind, personality, and culture after the fact. In these moments of total ego dissolution, Spirit may take on slight differences in qualities that generally include merging into a unitive experience of bliss, love, joy, creative power, or peace.

The essence of the experience of the Formless Spirit is the awareness that there is a source behind all things, an invisible mother essence, that gives birth to all things and yet is beyond all things. Interconnection is an idea that doesn't even make sense, since there are no two things to be connected in the moment of Formless Spirit. All is one, and there is an implied depth to reality far beyond imagination, Spirits, or subtle energy. Intellect cannot function on this level, only subtle feeling. "God" is now a force, a permeating transcendent essence. God as Formless Spirit has no discernment, no preferences, no reward or punishment. Good and evil dissolve into one creative universal power. Ideas, images, and anything else with a definite form is absolutely absent in the experience of the Formless Spirit. The core hallmark is the complete loss of duality and the felt sense of unity. It is a struggle to articulate the Formless Spirit in English. Hindu and Buddhist traditions have several complex and detailed inventories of higher states of consciousness and have created words like *Satchidananda* in Sanskrit which means, "Existence-consciousness-bliss." That is the Formless Spirit.

This extreme experience marks a transition into a distinct territory of spirituality that scholars have reserved for the true mystics over time. The experience of Formless Spirit is such a radical step beyond experiences that include or sustain personal awareness, and the definition and understanding of such a category of experiences remains complex. Truly only those who have had the experience can speak directly about it, and yet because of the nature of the experience there is an immediate understanding that all intellectual discussions will fall short. Scholars of mysticism and mystical experience have debated which spiritual states of consciousness can and should be called "mystical." Some would include all seven territories of the spiritual geography that we have explored. Others would say that only once a person begins to encounter the Formless Spirit do they truly enter the world and worldview of the mystic. It seems sensible to place your intent on having the experience. Engage in spiritual practices, fueled by deep longing but without expectation, and leave the analyses and debate to those whose care about such things.

Beyond Good and Evil

People who encounter this experience of Formless Spirit are certain that the true essence of The Sacred is without name or form. They experience that God has no religion; God is not an idea; God is beyond ideas; God is the Mysterious Force and Sacred Source, whose inner nature is love. The realization of this dimension of The Sacred causes many people to drop the use of the word God, because "God" as a word seems limited in time and space. I, however, still have not found a common Christian Western word, like *satchitananda* that carries layers of meaning, with nuance and feeling. I have found that Indigenous, ancient Jewish, and Islamic traditions have such words, but dedicate little or no energy in mainstream tradition for the discussion of this experience. A deeper value for, and understanding of, mystical states and the Formless

Experience is typically found in Eastern traditions such as in Hinduism, various Buddhist traditions and Taoism.

After this experience we understand that the ideas of good and evil, right and wrong, and all value-based judgments are empty of any true substance or universal meaning. They are all subsumed into one truth. This experience also accounts for why so many mystics have been ostracized and condemned in their traditions. After an experience of the Formless Spirit, we may become obsessed with The Sacred. God is clearly within us, not outside us. While the most accurate phrasing might be, "God is me," our outlawed mystics of the past have been run out of town for saying instead, "I am God." The statements are the same in the realm of Formless Spirit, but radically different to the everyday mind.

During and after an experience of Formless Spirit the idea of religion may seem oddly counterproductive. If radical enough, an encounter of Formless Spirit can even lead to people rejecting old roles, relationships, expectations, and habits. There is an implicit sense of freedom, and the sense that there can be no wrong decision, if made from the Flowering Heart of Spirit. Some people devote their lives to service, spiritual practice, and a spiritually oriented life after such an experience, for it seems the only logical choice.

It is also true that some people have this experience and soon after the "high," turn their attention back to the momentum and weight of the life they knew. Looking at the lives of my mentors, studying great masters and reflecting on the stories of my clients, I see that there sometimes is a connection between life experience and the ability to embrace the wisdom of the Formless Spirit. If a person has lived with a great deal of fear, attachment to ego, striving, and addiction to the material world, there can be a momentum that is hard to break, even after an experience of the Formless Spirit. Too often people who have tasted this experience lack the ability to fully integrate its meaning in their everyday life.

Mystics throughout history have experienced this divine awareness and used it to justify elitism, separatism, or the condemnation of those who do not see it. It is the irony of Sacred Vision gifted to a human ego. Because it is not always a common experience in communities of people, there can be a tendency to idolize the "mystic" and to socially use the gift of Awakening. Hitting "rock bottom" can help people to release limiting and conditioned ways of thinking and being in the world. But in a life in which there has been great perceived rewards for staying stuck in the mindset of power and control, it can be very difficult to absorb even the gifts of the Formless Spirit.

All Ways and None

There can be no predicting an experience of the Formless Spirit. No meditation, no drug, no ritual, no guru can promise this experience with certainty. Some people will be blessed with this encounter many times in life, and others may never truly experience it. This is not a statement of spiritual hierarchy, since a person who applies the wisdom of an experience of Truth and Beauty brings as much or more to the world as a person who has encountered the Formless Spirit and makes nothing of it.

Looking at the Indian traditions of yoga we see that these original systems were designed to cultivate this experience and awareness. Such systems are never as simple as most of us would like. Awakening to Formless Spirit was typically cultivated through a combination of things like diet, detoxification, physical postures, meditation, service work, certain attitudes, proper conduct, renunciation, devotion, chanting, and studying with a master. All of these elements and more might be integrated into the path of a true seeker of enlightenment.

The Buddha, as another example, taught that there are at least eight steps to achieving the experience of the Formless Spirit including specific protocol and practices relating to: understanding; thinking; speech; action; livelihood; effort; mindfulness; and concentration. Complex systems like these are found throughout the world and in many cases became the foundations of religious tradition. The heart of these systems is an intention to rid someone's life of distraction, spiritual congestion, or attachment, making practices more potent and the mind more available to radical states. If only it were remembered that any such system is designed to be a vehicle and not a resting place for the ego and the persona. The Twelve Master Paths explored in depth in my book *Return To The Sacred* identify the core practices that have liberated people in heart and mind throughout the ages, and can be a very helpful complement to this book.

Some traditions say this encounter of Formless Spirit comes only after time and the cultivation of spiritual practice; others say it is simply a matter of grace, that its occurrence and conditions are not for human logic to know. They would say to adopt a spiritual practice, to prepare yourself for the possibility. Commonly, we can say that experience of the Formless Spirit happens more likely:

- As a result of any extensive spiritual practice, such as those discussed in the book *Return to the Sacred*. Meditation and Ascetic practices stand out as ideal, but there is no rule.
- Around the time of a massive shock, trauma, or devastating loss, if supported with loving guidance, safe community and a spiritual context or container.
- In nature.
- In extremely strong ceremonies with culturally based and carefully supervised potent psychoactive "medicines."
- In the brief empty but lucid moment between waking and sleep.
- During very strict and deep detoxification and purification practices.

The Wisdom of Love

The experience of the Formless Spirit teaches us in a way that is very hard to explain to anyone who has not had a similar or related encounter. There is a quality of knowing that emerges from the felt-sense of unity and love. During such an experience there is typically no "aha!," no Sacred Voice, Divine Prophecy, or even a sense of learning anything in the moment. It is a receptive feeling. It is *just* the experience of a unitary mode of perception with the awareness that it is the source of all.

The lessons emerge from the experience, like seeds that slowly rise to our conscious mind upon our return. It is as if the experience is a catalyst for the flowering of wisdom, or that the experience itself encodes us with divine intelligence. Such an experience is often called awakening because the feeling is as if life, until that moment, had been an illusion of cause and effect, a distorted view of things. The experience of the Formless Spirit becomes a reference point; it holds implicit teachings on how to live, love and relate. It illuminates our capacity for peace, and our sense of divinity.

The Formless Spirit teaches us that there is a dimension to existence that is far beyond any of the things we preoccupy ourselves with in life. In this experience we encounter eternity, infinity, and an essence that can only be called Love. The Formless Spirit humbles the ego and awakens the spirit, pointing us beyond the origins of the world: you are born from love, you are sacred, you are an expression of the divine-bliss-consciousness.

Chapter Eight

The Experience of Pure Consciousness

When we begin to embrace even the idea
that there is nothing in existence but one pure existence,
our lives are transformed and so too
is the way we encounter the world.
At the core of this experience we learn that every-
thing in this world is sacred. Everything is divine,
by virtue of its divine origin, energy, and Sacred Source.
From this place we all become healers,
responsible for ourselves, each other, and this earth.

Somewhere Far Beyond

The core hallmark of the Pure Consciousness experience is the dissolving of self into what feels like the ultimate foundational energy or source of all reality—beyond thought or even perception. People have called this divine union, salvation, Oneness with God, samadhi, nirvana, total enlightenment, and many other things. It is a merging so complete that even the vast and infinite qualities that are sensed and perceived in the Formless Spirit are lost. The idea or sense of Love and Bliss are still dualistic, too formed and directed with intentionality and a sense of intelligence or human meaning. For me, and the literature and academic research on the topic supports this view, Pure Consciousness enters a realm of experience that hovers at the edge of existence itself. To me it feels like the last possible threshold between human mind and absolute vanishing into the most subtle field of existence that completely defies human knowing, understanding, or containment. Any shred of thought or self or even feeling extinguishes the experience immediately. It is more than egoless, it is self-less.

Those who remain permanently changed by and in contact with their experience of Pure Consciousness are classically known as mystics or "enlightened." These titles and qualifications have long been debated, and often a single spiritual experience does not qualify or "make" a person a mystic or wise master. Pure Consciousness experiences are rare, and are nearly always associated with permanent changes in perception and identity. To me, it seems impossible to have a Pure Consciousness experience and not feel absolutely convinced of our true spiritual nature and interconnection with all of existence. It is a radical encounter. Despite the fact that Pure Consciousness experiences are arguably the most universally uniform in nature, every instance must be considered uniquely.

Because the Pure Consciousness experience is more than rare, I would like to share my primary and most potent experience of this state and, as such, need to draw on a passage from the book, *Return to the Sacred*. While I'd rather share an original unpublished story, this excerpt remains perhaps my most precious and life-changing memory:

Within a few days, and after some hair-raising back roads that were more like hiking trails, I arrived. The place truly was extraordinary. It was extremely high in the Sierras, and from the ridges of stone and pine I could see far and wide into a vast range of mountains and valleys to the east. The air was notably different. It felt cleaner, thinner, crisper. There was a sense of isolation that was inescapable, and a secret thrill in the danger of a location beyond easy rescue. I set up my camp and began to plan my "great spiritual quest."

That first night after dinner, I decided to go for a walk in the moonlight. Nearby was a large area of exposed rock. It was a wonderfully smooth hilly outcrop that shone in the pale blue light of evening. I decided to take an old blanket with me so I could sit awhile in the moonlight. I felt that I needed to go and pray for guidance and help in the days to come; to take a last look at the world as I knew it.

I wanted to pray for the insight I had traveled so far to experience. I was growing nervous as to what I was committing myself, and so it seemed wise to take some time to be still and receive guidance. I wanted to be sure that my intention came from my heart and not my ego. I wanted to approach this next journey with reverence.

After a short walk I found myself at the foot of the bald rock outcropping I had seen from my camp. I walked up and over the smooth granite surface to the highest point. The stone face was glowing beneath the moonlight. I noticed that the moon was almost full. "Tomorrow would be a perfect night for my passage into spirit," I thought. I felt the rising force of fear as I wondered how many days I might have to spend in isolation: waiting, fasting, praying. I chased the thoughts from my head as I placed my folded blanket, like a pillow, on the ground.

I knelt down, facing the moon, and took a moment to relax. I knew that the passion I felt for my spiritual path was essential to cultivate the energy and focus that would be the gateway to a deeper awareness. I also knew that the desire to control the experience, or any emotion of anxiety or impatience could douse the very fire I was building. I took a deep breath.

Looking around, I could see the way the sky got darker and the stars appeared brighter, the further they were from the moon. The whole world around me was like a dark lake of deep shadows. Silhouettes of tall pines and patches of moonlight were scattered on stones and open spaces. I surrendered my senses to the beauty that flooded my vision. This was not a time for thoughts, or analysis. This was not a time for poetry or metaphor. I sat for awhile, and allowed myself to become still.

With each moment of silence, the energy of the world grew stronger. I could hear distant frogs by a pond; crickets; and the occasional night bird. I heard the twitch and rustle of the smallest animals searching for food among the pine needles and grasses. The sound of my breath was overwhelming, my heartbeat was like thunder. I wondered if the creatures would be scared off by the noise of my simple existence. I tried to soften my breath. I was floating on the slow depth of the night. The stillness was intense.

A surge of profound gratitude filled my body. How could I be so blessed to have this perfect moment on earth? Just to have the opportunity, the luxury to make such a quest, was a gift beyond measure. I remembered, abruptly, that I had come to pray, and took the time to bring my attention back to words, thoughts, and feelings.

I stared up at the moon, as if she could hear my soul, as if she was the face of The Sacred in this moment. The giant white-silver disc was more than a distant celestial body, but the very light and presence of God made manifest. I spoke my prayers of gratitude to her. I felt her loving attention, like a grandmother listening to her dear grandchild.

I gave thanks for the vastness of this world, honoring the four directions of the universe. I gave thanks for my family, for my life, for the one fragile moment I sat within. I forgot about the quest I had planned for the next day; I forgot about everything except the pure beauty of the moment and the infinite gratitude with which I was overflowing. And then, something happened.

As I stared at the moon, the world in my peripheral vision began to dissolve. I became aware of it for a moment, then blinked, and it all returned. I hadn't had anything to drink or any unusual foods. I had not taken drugs of any kind, nor had I any time prior. I was a bit confused by this experience. I felt so alert, it seemed my eyes were playing tricks on me. It was so odd it made me a bit nervous.

I tried to relax. Took a deep breath in and out. I returned my gaze to the moon—and the earth around me disappeared again. My eyes were open; I watched the sky as it too, slowly began to dissolve. I began to lose awareness of my body. Stars faded into the night sky; everything faded into the night sky until there was only an infinite field of dark and the sacred white light of God shining through the moon. My attention was transfixed. There was nothing in existence but that brilliant light in infinite space.

I became the light for a moment, a taste of Formless Spirit. It was vibration, life force, and joy. Only for a moment. Then unexpectedly, the moon also vanished. The sense of Divine Energy dissipated along with it.

Wide awake, eyes still wide open, there was absolutely nothing in the world to see. Everything had become one dark blue awareness. Then, my awareness of Nothing itself collapsed into an experience beyond experience. It was as if everything dissolved. Absolutely everything.

What happened next, I can only describe in retrospect. I experienced a moment without time or space, or content of any kind. There was no awe, no love, no unity, no presence. There was no God, no Web of Life or Sacred Voice; nothing. There was no Cosmic Self, no Spirit World, or Divine Energy. There was not even the experience of Love or Joy such as people encounter in the Formless Spirit. What followed was the experience of the cessation of all perception, while fully awake.

It was the vastness that embraces all that is and all that is waiting to be. Even words like eternity and infinity seem too small, for time and space are concepts that cannot even be held up to such a moment of pure consciousness.

There was only an Awareness so clear that there was no awareness at all. It was void, it was emptiness, it was more than infinite, it was eternal and beyond any dimensional quality. There was no self, no sub-ject, no ideas or feelings. Just pure existence: the absolute insubstantial presence-awareness of all being. It is pure silence, pure stillness. It is a radical emptiness that obliterated all self-awareness and consumed all reality. What it really is, is impossible to describe.

After what could have been moments, or hours, I suddenly became aware of the emerging presence of the sky. It was surfacing in my field of vision, as if rising out of a dark sea. At first I noticed a few stars, then the moon. There was not a cloud in the sky, nor had there ever been that night, but it was as if the moon and stars were materializing from thin air, or from behind a cloud. From Pure Consciousness, to resonant Love of Formless Spirit, the subtle vibrations and flow of Divine Energy, and on to the realm of Truth and Beauty, I felt like I was rising from the bottom of a great lake back to the surface of things.

Eventually, I became aware of the dark earth; soaring ponderosa pines, spruce, and the rocky hills atop this mountain. Finally, I gasped. I had completely forgotten my body, or that I had one. I don't even know if I had been breathing. It was only very slowly that I realized that there was an "I" sitting on a rock, praying in the night. It came as a shock to recognize my body again, as if the great void was more familiar than my own skin. It felt as if The Sacred Void was the true reality and all the emerging world was but a dream.

I began to move my tongue over my teeth as if for the first time ever. Each surface felt so extraordinary and unusual. I slowly flexed a finger with amazement. I felt alien to my own body. It was like a heavy robe, and I—my awareness, my spirit—was naked inside. I watched my thoughts form like clouds, brief rains of impulse and intention and then the body followed as willed. Slowly, as if recovering from amnesia, I recalled my name, and then, the awareness of my life and history gradually returned.

Every aspect of "who" I had been prior to that moment was clearly absurd. I had confused my "self" for my body, my family, my name, my journey, my emotions, and my thoughts. I thought all of those things were me. I called them "mine" as if I was inseparable from them. Now, I knew that in the one true reality, nothing is mine and nothing is me! Every mystic riddle I had read suddenly became clear to me. Everything made sense; now that nothing did. It was the most extraordinary moment of paradox.

I sat in a sober shock, as ideas and feelings filled my being. In that most transparent, translucent moment, I experienced myself as one with the true nature of being, the essence of God beyond form, thought or feeling. The world had become meaningless, and profound. Everything seemed broken and out of balance, yet everything felt perfect and peaceful. Every question in my life was answered. Every spiritual passage, scripture, and poem that I had encountered fell into place, like a jigsaw puzzle revealed before my inner vision. Yet, in the moment of Pure Consciousness there were no words, no ideas, no thoughts, no feelings.

The melting of the world around me into the nothingness was not a neurological delusion or a psychological illusion, but a revelation of the true essence of all things as expressions of One Spirit beyond concept. It was clear that this was showing something other than one system of things, but literally an essence and substance within and beyond everything and nothing. Afterwards, rather than an immediate feeling of "emptiness," what I felt instead was a profound fullness, and an exquisite sense of union and communion with the "Sacredness" that is absolutely all and everything.

This was a moment more incredible than divine love and connection, but true dissolution of all and identification with all, and all at once. That moment has shaped and touched all other moments of my life; it has become the foundation of my understanding of self and meaning, for in it there was no discovery, only a deep sense of knowing. It was an awakening to the Pure Consciousness that is the world, the watcher, the wisdom, the source, and something yet beyond all that. In the experience of Nothing, I felt as if I had realized everything.

Unlike the Formless Spirit, this experience is not only of the life behind life, and the energy within energy, it is the permeating Awareness that is everything, nothingness, and more. As I looked around, not only did I see and feel that all things were from the Divine Source, but I saw and felt that all things are divine. Every stone, every breath of wind, every thought and every moment. Everything is sacred.

When it was all over and I was present enough to move slowly, in a state of complete calm and peace, my body felt like it was gently vibrating to an imperceptible hum, and I began to make my way back to my tent. Still overwhelmed, I lay down, and an immense sense of gratitude emerged in me again—a joy and thankfulness for this experience, this revelation. It felt like everything in my heart and mind had been cleaned, washed clean. The feelings came so strongly, I burst into tears. I wept for a long time; my body shook with deep sobs of love and thankfulness. There were no thoughts to contain my joy, only feelings that exploded within me. That night the entire universe felt perfect, calm, and serene. It changed my life forever.

How Nothing Gives Us Something

The challenge of Pure Consciousness is that it is so difficult to discuss and yet its value is immense. In my own life, such experiences have been my most important and defining moments.

Reflecting on the other six types of spiritual experience, it seems that most could be inferred or intuited with enough information and imagery. This experience transcends all, which is its key characteristic. As I look to the ancient masters I've found that this sense that there is a state or stage beyond the Formless Spirit is not a delusion, but a globally and historically recorded experience.

Acharya Nāgārjuna was a great Buddhist spiritual teacher in India who lived sometime between the years of 150 and 250 C.E. Originator of the *Madhyamaka* (Middle Path) school of *Mahāyāna* Buddhism, many consider him the most important Buddhist, only surpassed by the Buddha. Many of his teachings focused on the experience of Pure Consciousness, which his tradition called *Sunyata,* or emptiness. In his wit and wisdom he summarized the essence of this experience by saying, "Whatever can be conceptualized is therefore relative, and whatever is relative is *Sunya,* empty. . . *Sunyata,* or the void, is shared by both *Samsara* [everyday life] and *Nirvana* [the Enlightened Mind]. Ultimately, *Nirvana* truly realized is *Samsara* properly understood." This shows us that the emptiness is the essence to understanding the material and the rational.

Paradox and Riddle— The Language of Pure Consciousness

Like all the great masters who have described the experience of Pure Consciousness, Nāgārjuna digresses into paradox and riddle. For no ordinary logic can capture the essence of this experience. The great Taoist text, the *Tao Te Ching,* says "The *Tao* that can be named is not the eternal *Tao.*" We see that the impossible language and concepts our spiritual traditions have used for God and the Awakened State are not always lazy philosophies or hypotheses, but struggling attempts to express the experience of Pure Consciousness, in which we realize the nature of all things. Seng-t`san, known as the Third Zen Patriarch, lived in China in the 7th Century. He is credited for the earliest and one of the most brilliant explanations of Zen Buddhist thought. A short passage from his key work, The Faith Mind, affirms the puzzle and prize of Pure Consciousness.

When no discriminating thoughts
arise, the old mind ceases to exist.
When thought objects vanish, the
thinking-subject vanishes:
As when the mind vanishes, objects vanish.

Things are objects because of the subject (mind):
the mind (subject) is such because of things
(object). Understand the relativity of these two and
the basic reality: the unity of emptiness. In this
Emptiness the two are indistinguishable and each
contains in itself the whole world.

What's It Like?

Much like experiences of Divine Energy and Formless Spirit, Pure Consciousness experiences involve the dissolving of self-awareness, and the experience of non-dual, continuous, united, reality and perception. It's a subtle point, but the Pure Consciousness experience is not of connection *to* all things, nor did it *feel* like Love or a revelation, in the way these things occur in other "types" of spiritual experiences, like Divine Energy and Formless Spirit. The experience of Pure Consciousness is a direct self-realization of the profoundly incomprehensible nature of the origin of all things. In many ways it is like the experience of Formless Spirit, and teaches us of the unitary reality of life in the most profound way.

During a moment of Pure Consciousness the material world is revealed as being just the tiniest particle of what truly exists within and beyond all things. Its substance could be called a Force, what I can only call "The Sacred" or "God"—a Force so beyond comprehension that its greatest dimensions lay eternally beyond the material world, and yet resonating within every obvious and subtle sense we possess as human beings. A return from Pure Consciousness *with* ego and personhood fully intact is as difficult as it is to return without them all together. Ego and personhood are necessary aspects of the human condition, but they can change and evolve dramatically from what we have come to assume. Somehow, over time, a new balance between our identification with being and non-being must be struck.

In that moment of return from Pure Consciousness, I knew as certainly as I know night from day, that the Divine Silent Depth of God is the one true reality that no one person, culture, religion, or science will ever control or define. The Divine Silent Depth of God *is* the seeker, the scientist, the mystery, the chaos, and the patterns and wisdom of life's design. Things are not just connected, they are one Sacred thing. This life-changing experience, which is ancient and universal among cultures, reveals that God/Consciousness/The Great Mystery is *everything* and much, much more. All form, all dimensions, all planes of existence are possible because of this one Being Beyond Being: the Spirit that holds all, and is all.

Ineffable: Something from Nothing

The experience of Pure Consciousness is the most profoundly extraordinary experience and the most impossible to articulate. Many people and mystics are attracted to other states because they are more accessible and can be more "fun," more familiar, and more self-directed. This experience of The Sacred leaves you completely vulnerable and without any parameters of meaning or identity, except the pure voice of the soul and spirit that live within you. When you return from such an experience, the spontaneous honoring of the spiritual heart becomes the only guide. In his book, *Nature, Man and Woman*, the brilliant Alan Watts does an incredible job at expressing the way we may live from the wisdom that Pure Consciousness teaches.

Many times before I had the distinct awareness that there is a Sacred Presence or Divine Spirit within everything. I had deeply felt that all things are a creation of God—the Source Energy. During many moments in nature I could "see" and feel a grand design that spoke of something much greater. But this was a totally different sense of knowing. After this moment, somehow it was clear how totally and radically *beyond* all things is the eternal source of life, while being completely immanent and intimate in all things. This is the one spiritual experience that I am aware of in which the transformation is typically lasting and permanent.

The Formless Spirit has been the core reality of the mystical traditions and the core experience of the mystics. Pure Consciousness was often seen as the "highest state" in many traditions and is often associated with "enlightened" or "ascended masters." Naturally, I don't see much value in a firm sense of hierarchy in spiritual development, nor in comparison or competition. Even among those who have truly realized Pure Consciousness, there are stages and levels of integration.

Western traditions have tended not to focus on this direct realization of The Sacred as a possibility or desired outcome for "ordinary people." Instead, those who attain such states and stages are seen as prophets, saints, or masters to follow as a means to acquire God's favor. Traditions built on hierarchy and control favor dedication and obedience to religious leaders as representatives of God and generally discourage people from seeking the obliteration of self, ego, and identity in fusion of awareness with The Sacred.

The ancient Eastern philosophies had great regard and ambition for states such as Pure Consciousness. Referred to as *turiya* in some traditions, there remains a deep understanding of the value and power of such an experience to liberate a person from fear, stress, worry, and suffering. Perhaps because the path is steep and can require great sacrifice, many people seek practices that allow them to defer the responsibility of Pure Consciousness to teachers, masters, saints, and sages.

Do Nothing

The idea of creating an experience of Pure Consciousness is an oxymoron, a self-contradicting statement. The complexity lies in that a sincere longing to realize the depth and truth of whatever you call "The Sacred" is a critical condition to engage. Deep heartfelt willingness, commitment to a path, and surrender in gratitude are all elements common to tales of Pure Consciousness. Yet, a breath away from these qualities lies attachment, expectation, ego, and all the other impediments to Pure Awareness.

In the depths of spiritual awakening you can take nothing—no ego, no questions, no time or space. It happens to you, it becomes you. That is when you realize that *you are it!* In a moment of pure consciousness, your everyday sense of self, melts like an ice cube in an infinite ocean. There is no capacity to differentiate your "self" from the great ocean of being. Much like the Formless Spirit, it can be said that experiences of Pure Consciousness come gradually through spiritual practice, progressive experience, and guidance. Or, it can be said that such an experience is a simple matter of grace and divine blessing: it will happen when it is meant to happen.

There is no way to predict when an experience of Pure Consciousness may occur. It is my sense that this is the most uncommon of the seven and the most difficult to predict. I do not, however, feel it is the most important or best. A soul may be healed by any state or experience. Enlightenment is not just an experience, it is also a *stage* of consciousness. Enlightenment is about a quality of personal maturity. It is the consciousness with which you live your life.

Any of the seven sacred experiences may help you to create the shift in your life and spirituality that you seek. In fact, some of the simplest and most ordinary experiences, such as Truth and Beauty, can incrementally move a soul along the path to the fullest awakening you can imagine. This is why all spiritual practices and all seven spiritual experiences are important to the healing and transformation of individuals and the world.

Changed Forever

It is important to be aware of the way the experience of Pure Consciousness changes people and what it teaches them. Even just the knowledge of these things can inform and transform the way we understand life and all the other types of spiritual experience. When we begin to embrace even the idea that there is nothing in existence but that One Pure Existence, our lives are transformed and so too is the way we encounter the world. Qualities like judgment, comparison, conflict, greed, addiction, and violence, all wither and fade from the life of one who has cut out their roots.

Much of life's suffering lies in the illusions and conclusions about our separateness from the world. Feeling cut off or divided, we seek power and control over others. In the absence of our divine essence we believe the stories and identity we have received through our family of origin and life's successes and failures. Life becomes conditional without the awareness of our unity. When we find disagreement we move to conflict instead of collaboration, or from mutual growth to defence. This changes when we *feel* our unity with all things and *see* the presence of The Sacred in all things.

At the core of this experience, what I learned/felt/knew is that everything in this world is sacred. Everything is divine, by virtue of its divine origin and Sacred Source. I recognized that I would have a life full of thoughts, emotions, actions, and dramas, but in the end, those realities would be transient, thinly veil-like expressions of something eternal and most profound. It was like becoming invincible and totally humbled in the same moment. It was life's greatest gift, and a lifelong path to fully realize it.

From the place of knowing that all things are born of a common source it reveals the limits of judgment, duality and even your sense of good and evil. Rather than living in a world in which your actions are based on personal or social projections of right and wrong, you will seek to find or create goodness in all and work towards the good as you know it always.

In the deepest connection to Spirit you can access a new source of choice and decision making. In the mindset of Deep Spirit you oppose violence because it dishonors Creation and the Sacred gift. You will see that violence against anything is destruction of the Sacred and yourself. You feel as if you are are hurting yourself. When you see the world as Sacred, then you naturally take action to bring peace to the world in every way you are aware and every way you feel empowered or pulled. Honoring of life and the recognition of Spirit in all things becomes a way of being. Peace and healing become universal responsibilities, not just the privilege of some people, groups, or nations.

When you see all things as Sacred—even the terrible things in life— it allows you to fully recognize them without pushing them away. A great Shona African spiritual teacher and mentor of mine, Mandaza Kandemwa, always says, "An enemy is one whose story you have not heard yet." By this he shares the same truth: division creates more division, peace brings peace. When we see our enemy as Sacred we will finally learn how to disarm them and ourselves. We will see their pain, their weakness, and we will understand them as we understand ourselves. The problems in life begin the moment we claim that anything is *not* Sacred. How do we draw those lines? Who draws them?

The experience of Pure Consciousness doesn't leave with a desire to be righteous or right. It empowers us to surrender to each moment, to be fully present and connected to the unity of things. From this place we all become healers, responsible for ourselves, each other, and this earth.

The Eternal Seed

Looking at my own experience I recall the way it resonated within me days afterward. I felt as if I had been hit with the vibration of an atomic blast. I had to live simply, sleep often, and rest in nature. Insights simply came, one after the other, like the birth of new life on earth after a flood recedes.

For years afterward I traveled the world seeking further understanding of the pathways, technologies and philosophies of the Sacred. New experiences came and the same radiant seed of experience continued to unfold. The great Master Paths have helped me to not only activate new encounters of The Sacred, but to cultivate and refine myself, so that I may live what I have learned. At times it has been extremely challenging to heal my emotional-self, release my ego, and manage my physical reality so that I can live in harmony with this mystic vision. I have had jobs that required that I worked with people who could not care less about Pure Consciousness, and I have had friends, lovers, and family like anyone else. Congruency is the key. Surrender, trust, gratitude, and dedication are the elements that have helped me to nurture the Seed of Pure Awareness that was planted that day. One thing is most certain: this is a journey that has no end.

Conclusion

The Heart of One and All

"Though my soul may set in darkness, it will rise in perfect light;
I have loved the stars too fondly to be fearful of the night."

~ Sarah Williams

Crazy Horse dreamed and went into the world where
there is nothing but the spirits of things.
That is the real world that is behind this one,
and everything we see here is something like a shadow
from that world . . . It was this vision that gave him
his great power, for when he went into a fight,
he had only to think of that world to be in it again, so
that he could go through anything and not be hurt.

~ Black Elk

The Voyage

As we come to the end of this exploration of the dimensions of our wider and wilder world, do not let feelings of either satisfaction or dissatisfaction over the style of this book decide what is next for you. The book is just a map, a tool, a reference to something waiting for you. The worlds of Spirit and Insight are ever-present and all around. Each day, each moment, we live a step away from an experience of life that is full of wonder, hope, and deep connection. This is not, however, a journey of the mind. The traveler into the world of Spirit becomes an explorer of the heart. For as we travel deeper into the greater dimensions of this world, what we discover is that we are more interconnected, interdependent, and interrelated than we could ever have imagined.

Spiritual experience is not about acquiring super-powers or a metaphysical superiority to others. Spiritual experiences aren't trophies either, like the practices and philosophies that lead us to them. Each spiritual experience is pointing us somewhere deeper: to the Oneness of our world.

To realize that we are born into a Living Energy Universe is to realize that we are much more than this life or what we have yet been shown. Spiritual experiences remind us that we are greater than anything that has ever been said or done to us. No matter how broken or depleted we may feel, there is always an abundant and vital dimension to who we are that remains untouchable.

To begin the journey into the fullness of our universe is to begin a journey that never ends, is always personal, and always has more to reveal.

Rocky Shores—
Important Precautions and Warnings

A deep willingness to release what we know for a new experience of self can change and challenge a lot in one person's life. Spiritual experiences can be the root of great healing, self-love, the release of shame, and the blossoming of compassion. We must not, however, assume all spiritual experiences will be easy, comfortable, or even have a positive outcome. Too often spiritual experiences can lead to struggle and a loss of meaning and not always the easy and joyful fulfilment shared throughout this book. In life, we tend to see more of what we are looking *through* than what we are looking *at*: meaning, our culture, emotional history, personality, assumptions about life and self are all factors that can shape our reaction to a non-ordinary state.

Many mental health conditions, addictions, or a history of trauma can be incredibly supported or even "healed" through deep spiritual experience, but they *can also be exacerbated and made worse* if there is no safe container of meaning, community support, and direct guidance available. For people living with complex trauma or mental health conditions such as dissociative disorders, schizophrenia, and borderline personality disorder, spiritual experiences can be hard to distinguish from unhealthy episodes or even personal crisis. Naturally, some spiritual states foster more stability and "real world" grounding, while others can truly test a person's sense of reality.

As with any potent medicine or powerful practice, spiritual experiences should be approached with respect, with care, thoughtfulness, and with good guidance and timing. To assist you in how you approach spiritual practice and experience please consider the following questions. You should be able to answer yes to at least three of the five questions below:

Questions

1. Am I seeking this today to bring love and wisdom to my life and not only to escape discomfort?
2. Do I have a person or people I trust who I can go to with questions about my experiences and who I will go to if I feel confused or unwell after a spiritual practice?
3. Do I have an integrated (well-functioning) community, support group, family or tradition to support me and help me make sense of whatever I may face, or at least support me to find answers?
4. Is my doctor likely to be comfortable with me doing this?
5. Have I practiced the basic skills of mindfulness, meditation, and self-observation so that I can truly receive and not react to whatever I may encounter?

An Endless Journey

It is my distinct experience, obvious by now, that spirituality is not about belief or choice any more than physicality is. We all have a body. Our bodies differ in so many ways, yet there is no denying that human life requires a physical element to thrive. Some people may be born with physical prowess and aptitudes that others don't have; some people practice and develop physical ability and skill; and of course, others must focus on managing illness or injury—but we all have a physical dimension to life on earth. In just the same way, we all have a spiritual dimension. Each person lives by a conscious or unconscious worldview, a set of values and each must answer the questions: what matters most, what relationships are important, and who am I really? These three questions form the foundation by which all of our experiences are framed, understood and responded to. As these three questions evolve and mature within us our relationship to self, health, resilience, and community grows.

The spiritual journey, no matter how magical, mystical, psychedelic or fantastical it may seem or sound, is the most practical and useful life process we can undertake. I have worked in research, consulting, and leadership in places as diverse as hospitals, prisons, Fortune 100 companies, resorts, urban communities, and remote rural settings and in every case, but one, it has been abundantly clear that people with meaningful relationships, a strong sense of self-awareness and self-understanding, tools for coping with stress and a framework of thinking that allows them to manage emotions and life's challenges with presence and purpose are always more likely to heal faster, live longer, and find some important form of success at work. The one exception I experienced was a Wall Street workplace where extreme competition was rewarded, high rates of burnout were overlooked, and the company thrived by short term gain and low ethical standards.

Naturally, anyone can excel for a short time without a spiritual path or worldview. People and companies do it all the time. True personal success, with resilience, joy, and sustainability eventually needs to be rooted in something deeper than self-interest or a divisive way of living.

We are born from, and into, a universe in which all things are interconnected. Whether you explain this profound interconnection as dumb luck or a higher order at work, it is what it is. We are already woven into a world of oneness. Researcher and journalist Scott Kaufman reviewed a number of studies that investigated the prevalence and impact of a "oneness" worldview. In the magazine *Scientific American*, he wrote:

People who believe that everything is fundamentally one differ in crucial ways from those who do not. In general, those who hold a belief in oneness have a more inclusive identity that reflects their sense of connection with other people, non-human animals, and aspects of nature that are all thought to be part of the same "one thing." This has some rather broad implications.

Kaufman goes on to discuss how people who "believe in oneness," regardless of culture or religion are far more prone to hopefulness, a feeling of connection with life, a growth-mindset, and a greater capacity for compassion and a sense of purpose. The outcomes of a rich spiritual life that continues to evolve and remains in dialogue with lived experience are absolutely life affirming and health promoting.

Mystics and sages of the past experienced spiritual states without the context of global science, cross-cultural knowledge, or the internet. Today's spiritual explorers have the opportunity to cultivate an integrative/integrated understanding of self and life, much along the lines of what Ken Wilber lays out in his books *Integral Life Practice* and *Integral Meditation*. This means that a person who pursues the gifts and insights of spiritual practice can apply their experiences to all areas of life and not fall prey to the old world modes of using spiritual experience to feed the ego or to justify one's own separated sense of cultural superiority. A true open heart and mind will find that spiritual experience is exactly what prepares and inspires you to face the chaos and crisis of the modern world with equanimity, optimism, and a willingness to engage and make a difference.

The Last Story (For Now)

There is an old story that has long been used in religious and spiritual traditions. There are different versions and characters but the same basic structure and conclusion. The most popular version is known as "the frog in the well" and is believed to have originated in China in the fourth century B.C.E. Some refer to a collection of fables and teaching stories and some refer to a great philosopher and the name Zhuāng Zi has been attributed to both. While the origin is unclear the story is not.

It is said, that once there was a frog who lived at the bottom of a well. He was born there and lived his whole life hopping among the craggy stones that made the walls of the well and dipping in to the water to find bugs and his daily drink. One day a curious turtle passed by and noticed the well, and then the frog.

"What are you doing down there?" she shouted.

"This is my home, I live here," the frog replied.

"Why don't you come up here," said the turtle. "There are lakes and rivers, long grasses, a big beautiful sky, so much to eat and a vast, endless ocean."

The frog laughed himself into hysterics.

"You must be totally insane," he said to the turtle. "Such things cannot and do not exist. I don't know what you see, but surely you are a fool. You should come down here and see how well I live."

The turtle could not climb into the well, not with her great, big shell, and much less with her simple body. She wished the frog well and went on her way.

The next season was hot and the rains did not come at all. The well dried up. The frog waited and waited for a change but none came. The frog considered what the turtle had once told him but was too afraid to face what surely would be a great disappointment and maybe even a tragic fate. The frog slowly began to starve as the water did not return and the bugs had all gone away.

One day, now sensing his own inevitable death in the well, the frog slowly, carefully made his way up the rocky sides of the well. Finally, in a true moment of terror, the frog reached the edge of the well, the light was blinding and the world was loud. His senses were overwhelmed. Slowly, however, his eyes and ears began to adjust.

His racing heart slowed down and he looked around in amazement. Though his well had dried up there was still water in the new world around him. The flowing river, the small but rippling lake, and in the distance the great, great ocean. There were flowers and bugs of astounding variety.

What the frog thought was an impossible story, and a likely certain death, turned out to be the most amazing opportunity of his life.

Only You

Like the frog in the story above, each one of us lives within the limits of our minds, our conditioning, and the parameters of our experience. To dive deep into the world of spiritual experience is to dive deep into what it means to be fully alive and fully human. The more we explore beyond the world of ordinary senses and states of awareness, the more we can bring a deep sense of mystery, wonder, interconnection, and calm to all we do. As we learn to transcend day to day experience through spiritual awakening, ironically, day to day experience becomes more fulfilling, more precious and more intimate.

Thinking and philosophizing about spirituality is a great way to stay stuck in a life of control, reaction, or escape. Trusting in the same force that has been shaping our universe for billions of years to connect with and express to you, for you, and through you, is the beginning of a life that is filled with reward, surprise, and a peace that can never be shaken.

A spirit-centered life objectifies our own reactions and knows to listen deeply to our innermost self, each other, and our natural world. The same talents and tools that will help you to grow comfortable with spiritual states are the very same talents and tools you will need to face the world with courage, grace, and kindness. It remains true, that there is no greater teacher than life. Today and through these stories, however, what changes is our definition of life, and just how much it can teach us. Life is infinitely more than we can see or feel in any one moment. Our human world is but a flash of reflected light on a passing wave. To know this is more than humbling, it frees us from the need to be anything more than who and what we are right now. To glimpse the spiritual world is to be assured that each day is a true and profound gift.

What lies ahead cannot be passed on like a book or a practice. What awaits you is something only you can know for yourself, as yourself. As you discover the extraordinary vastness and magical complexity of the inner world, you will, in time, fall in love with life again, and as if for the first time ever.

First and Last

In closing, I can only invite you, one last time, to look to the spiritual world and all those sincere and surrendered traditions, teachers, masters, sages, lovers, and heart-centered, whole-life leaders of change, just as you look to the stars on a dark and brilliant night. They can help. What they left behind can help. Like children that have unwillingly been torn away from their homes, these wild seekers and guides have tried to remember what it was once like to live In Spirit, and have shared what they have found for our wellbeing. Regardless of how eventually misunderstood or misguided they may have been, it is worth sorting through.

Although this whole book is about other worlds and magical energy, mystical moments and spiritual forces, in the end, what we have is *this life* and a very human experience. We hurt, we hope, we heal, and we seek a way to feel like we are enough—like we belong. When I look back over what we have shared, what fills my heart is not only the great blessing of God and Spirits, but the unspeakable beauty of the human search for love and meaning. I remember the gritty earth and smell of summer grass during vision quests held with all the love of a community supporting me with ceremonies and prayers, sacred fires, and late nights watching the skies. I see the magnificent dark skin and flashing smiles of far-away faces, children who ran beside me on my way to new villages and their healers. I feel the hand-smoothed stones of the Western Wall in Jerusalem, every crack filled with prayers and wishes. I see the glowing domes of mosques, the towering glory of redwoods, the massive shadows of whale sharks, jungles, cities, late nights and early mornings, family among strangers, language upon languages, and ancient pathways passed on, day after day, for thousands of years, sometimes at the risk of death itself. I have been a very privileged, and fortunate traveler.

Ours is a beautiful world and yours is a beautiful life. Don't let the pain of everyday life and the division that seems to take root everywhere overshadow the radiant power of your unique way of being alive. The world needs you in your fullest expression. We may not have long left as a species, but a return to a greater vision of life, love, and wisdom can only be good for all of us. It just might buy us some time and provide the tools most needed. To remember our interconnection with all things is to restore a trust in the ability for Existence itself to guide, protect, and nourish us is an adventure worth more than can ever be shared in words.

"Let everything happen to you
Beauty and terror
Just keep going
No feeling is final."

~ Rainer Maria Rilke

Recommended Reading

I have been very fortunate to have had the time, means, and privilege to read a mountain of books on spiritual growth and the spiritual world. With a doctoral degree in comparative religion, ordination as an Interfaith Minister with a concentration on spiritual counseling, and a life-long passion to understand my own spiritual experiences and the transformative process of others, I have collected a massive library of resources covering a wide range of interrelated topics. Having made this clear for context only, there are only a select few books I have consistently recommended over the years.

It is difficult to reduce my recommendations to a handful, since every book written carries its own gift and value. In my opinion, nevertheless, the following books were formative for me and are perhaps essential in the collection of any spiritual seeker—advanced or just beginning. I hope you find the time to explore and enjoy adding some of these to your collection.

General Spiritual Development with a Psychological Dimension

Dass, Ram and Paul Gorman. *How Can I Help?* New York: Knopf, 1985.

Dass, Ram. *Polishing the Mirror.* Boulder, CO: Sounds True, 2014.

Grof, Stan and Christina. *Spiritual Emergency.* New York: TarcherPerigee, 1989.

Kornfield, Jack. *A Path With Heart and The Wise Heart.* New York: Bantam, 1993.

Walsh, Roger and Frances Vaughan, eds. *Paths Beyond Ego.* New York: TarcherPerigee, 1993.

Ancient Texts and Collections

Mitchell, Stephen, ed. *The Enlightened Heart.* New York: Harper Perennial, 1993.

Mitchell, Stephen, ed. *The Enlightened Mind.* New York: Harper Perennial, 1993.

Oman Maggie, ed. *Prayers for Healing.* Newbury Port, MA: Conari Press, 2000.

Tzu, Lao with Mitchell, Stephen Mitchell, ed. *Tao Te Ching.* New York: Harper Perennial Modern, 2006.

Indigenous Insights

Kalweit, Holger. *Dreamtime & Inner Space.* Boulder, CO: Shambhala, 1988.

Kimmerer, Robin Wall. *Braiding Sweet Grass.* Minneapolis, MN: Milkweed Editions, 2015.

Mitchell, Sherri. *Sacred Instructions.* Berkeley, CA: North Atlantic Books, 2018.

Spiritual Insight through Cultural Lenses

Hesse, Herman. *Siddhartha.* New York: Bantam, Reissue edition, 1981.

Yogananda, Paramahansa. *Autobiography of a Yogi.* Los Angeles, CA: Self-Realization Fellowship, 1971.

Books by Jonathan H. Ellerby

Return to the Sacred. Carlsbad, CA: Hay House, 2009.

Inspiration Deficit Disorder. Carlsbad, CA: Hay House, 2010.

The Promise of Paradise. Carlsbad, CA: Hay House, 2012.

About the Author

Jonathan H. Ellerby, Ph.D., has spent more than 35 years dedicated to the personal, professional, and academic exploration of spirituality, healing, and consciousness. Throughout his journey, he has traveled the world meeting and studying with spiritual teachers from more than 40 cultural traditions. Jonathan has a doctoral degree in comparative religion and an ordination as an interfaith minister. He has worked as a healer, teacher, and consultant with individuals and groups in settings as diverse as hospitals, major corporations, prisons, community groups, conferences, and some of the world's leading holistic health resorts. He was a pioneering spiritual program director for Canyon Ranch Health Resorts and led the innovation of many other spiritual programs and projects. His work and training have taken him deeply into the worlds of indigenous healing, corporate culture, integrative medicine, and nature-based travel.

Jonathan is the author of *Return to the Sacred, Inspiration Deficit Disorder,* and *The Promise of Paradise.*

For more information see: **www.jonathanellerby.com**

Confident Empath
by Suzanne Worthley

Exploring different ways one can feel and perceive energies from human energy fields, places, paranormal situations, and across dimensions, this comprehensive guide offers advanced strategies to energetically protect yourself, heal energetically, and discover self-empowerment.

ISBN 9-781-64411-755-2

The Spiritual Awakening Guide
by Mary Mueller Shutan

Addressing every step of the spiritual journey to enlightenment, this pragmatic, clear guide highlights different types of spiritual awakenings and explains characteristics, possible challenges, and ways to navigate the twelve layers that cover an awakened state. The focus lies on facilitating a graceful awakening process that allows us to continue leading a grounded, earth-bound life with heightened spiritual awareness.

ISBN 9-781-84409-671-8